AMERICAN BEARS

Theodore Roosevelt and friend relaxing during the 1905 bear hunt in Colorado. Courtesy of the Theodore Roosevelt Collection, Harvard College Library.

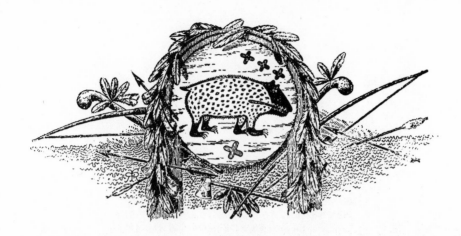

AMERICAN BEARS

Selections from the Writings
of

Theodore Roosevelt

edited and with an introduction
by

Paul Schullery

foreword by

John A. Gable
Executive Director
Theodore Roosevelt Association

Published by Colorado Associated University Press
Boulder, Colorado 80309
ISBN 0-87081-135-5 (Cloth) and 0-87081-136-3 (Paper)
Library of Congress Card Catalog Number 82-071701
Designed by Michael Haller

*This book is dedicated to the good work
of the Boone and Crockett Club
and
the Theodore Roosevelt Association*

Books by Paul Schullery
Old Yellowstone Days *(editor)*
The Bears of Yellowstone
The Orvis Story *(with Austin Hogan)*
The Grand Canyon: Early Impressions *(editor)*
Freshwater Wilderness: Yellowstone Fishes and their World *(with John D. Varley)*
American Bears: Selections from the Writings of Theodore Roosevelt *(editor)*

CONTENTS

ACKNOWLEDGMENTS

John Gable, executive director of the Theodore Roosevelt Association, encouraged me in this project from its beginning, and as the book began to take shape he provided considerable assistance with specific research requests. Because of this support and his eminence as director of the Theodore Roosevelt Association I am particularly pleased that he has provided the book with a thoughtful foreword.

Wallace Finley Dailey, curator of the Theodore Roosevelt Collection at Harvard College Library, provided invaluable assistance and guidance to that most excellent collection, making my research even more enjoyable.

My introduction benefited greatly from readings by John Gable, Stephen Herrero of Calgary, Alberta, and A. Starker Leopold of Berkeley, California.

The staffs of Mark Skinner Library, Manchester, Vermont, and the Yellowstone Park Research Library, Yellowstone Park, Wyoming, helped me track down a number of items that I could not have found otherwise.

Finally, I am grateful to a prominent historian of the late nineteenth century. Neither his numerous books on historical subjects nor his equally numerous and perhaps better known books on outdoor life are as well remembered as they might be had he not also been president of the United States. I hope that this "new" book by Theodore Roosevelt helps in some small way to balance our understanding of his remarkable character; just as we remember the big stick but forget the Nobel Peace Prize, we remember the trophy room but forget the scientific acclaim he earned as one of the greatest "faunal naturalists" in American history.

FOREWORD

Here is a collection of pieces on the American bear, originally published between 1885 and 1908, written by the man who was the twenty-sixth president of the United States.

The naturalist John Burroughs said of his friend Theodore Roosevelt: "Roosevelt was a many-sided man and every side was like an electric battery. Such versatility, such vitality, such thoroughness, such copiousness, have rarely been united in one man." TR was indeed something of a "Renaissance man," and it is this many-sided quality as much or more than anything else about him that makes him one of the most interesting Americans who ever lived.

Theodore Roosevelt (1858–1919) was historian, naturalist, hunter, rancher, soldier, explorer, prolific writer on diverse subjects, conservationist, and, of course, politician and president. Two of TR's works on history, *The Naval War of 1812* (1882) and his study of the westward movement, *The Winning of the West* (4 volumes: 1889–1896), are regarded as classics. Roosevelt also wrote biographies of Thomas Hart Benton (1887), Gouverneur Morris (1888), and Oliver Cromwell (1900), as well as a history of New York City (1891). As a naturalist, he studied, hunted, and wrote about wildlife in North America, Africa, and South America. TR was a rancher in the Dakota Territory in the 1880s, and his books about the West, *Hunting Trips of a Ranchman* (1885), *Ranch Life and the Hunting Trail* (1888), and *The Wilderness Hunter* (1893), helped fix the images of cowboy life and the "wild West" that have come down to us. As a soldier, he won fame as the Colonel of the Rough Riders in the Spanish-American War. As an explorer, he put a river on the map—the "Rio Roosevelt" or "Rio Teodoro" in Brazil. Roosevelt was also a man of letters who published over fifty volumes and hundreds of newspaper and magazine articles on a myriad of topics. He was one of the original members of the National Institute of Arts and Letters, one of the first fifteen elected to the American Academy of Arts and Letters, and president of the American Historical Association. As a politician, TR was a major figure in American public life for nearly forty years, serving as New York State Assemblyman, U.S. Civil Service Commissioner, New York City Police Commissioner, Assistant Secretary of the Navy, Governor of New York, vice president and president of the United States, and, in his later years, leader of his own political party. As the twenty-sixth president of the United States, 1901–1909, TR busted trusts and promoted federal regulation of big business, built the Panama Canal, won the Nobel Peace Prize, and did more for conservation than any American leader before or since. Roosevelt's presidential record on conservation includes the establishment of five national parks; the preservation of eighteen natural sites, such as Devil's Tower in Wyoming, Muir Woods in California, and the Grand Canyon in Arizona; the increase of federal forest reserves by over 300%; and the creation of the first federal wildlife refuges.

This book—a book about bears—shows several facets of the many-sided Roosevelt which, with the passage of time, have been put into the shadow by his importance as a political leader. In these selections, TR displays his talents as a writer, his interest in natural history, the wide range of his knowledge and experience, and his love of outdoor life. We see TR as the apostle of what he called the "strenuous life," and we can feel his love of adventure, his keen curiosity, and his dynamism.

TR was a great story-teller, and he had some great bear stories to tell. He was a vivid writer with a sharp sense of detail, and he was fascinated by nearly everything that came his way. Roosevelt's descriptions of bear life are valuable both as literature and as natural history. On one level, this book is simply good reading. On other levels, *American Bears* reveals much about the wilderness, wildlife, and a great man who interacted with both.

In addition to TR's writings, *American Bears* contains Paul Schullery's informative and perceptive "Introduction" to Roosevelt's pieces. Schullery fills gaps in our knowledge and understanding of Theodore Roosevelt as outdoorsman, naturalist, and nature-writer. With the very notable exception of Paul Russell Cutright's *Theodore Roosevelt the Naturalist*, published in 1956, relatively little has been written about these important aspects of TR's life and career. Schullery's "Introduction" addresses the question of "Roosevelt's hunting as historical scandal," evaluates TR's competence and importance as a naturalist, and looks at TR's standing as a nature-writer.

TR's hunting offends the sensibilities of many people today, but Schullery shows that this interpretive problem derives in large measure from a failure to understand TR's times, the conditions of outdoor life he faced, and his philosophy of nature. "If by some people's standards today (or even in his own time), hunting is morally unjustifiable," Schullery writes, "Roosevelt's pursuit of that sport was not the result of a lack of a firm moral code; it was instead the result of a different moral code." Schullery helps us to know and appreciate that code, whether ultimately we choose to agree with it or not. Schullery places TR's writings on the bear in the context of natural history in Roosevelt's day, and concludes that TR's contributions were greater than those of any single writer before 1909. As an able and informed field naturalist, TR, says Schullery, stands in the great tradition of John James Audubon. On the lighter side, Schullery also tells us the story of how TR became the father of the "Teddy Bear." (Fun is never far away when one is talking about TR.) Finally, Schullery discusses TR's stature as a nature-writer, concluding that he stands with some of the best. In sum, Paul Schullery's "Introduction" adds a great deal to the value, enjoyment, and interest to be found in this book.

Paul Schullery says that Roosevelt's hunting and nature books have "endured," and the publication of this present volume of selections from TR's writings seems proof of that. Sit back, then, and prepare to immerse yourself in a long-ago world of bears and men and wild places.

John Allen Gable
Executive Director
Theodore Roosevelt Association
Oyster Bay, New York

The most famous variation of the Clifford Berryman cartoon that inspired the Teddy Bear.

INTRODUCTION

For most of us it is difficult to appreciate the magnitude of Theodore Roosevelt's achievements as a naturalist and hunting writer; his greater, historical, stature keeps intruding. Even when reading his more enervating (and always a little romantic) adventure tales, one never entirely escapes the knowledge that one is audience to a president of the United States. Roosevelt's political significance tends to obscure his place as one of the leading big game authorities of his day, his place as a gifted and versatile naturalist in other fields, and his position as one of the most capable nature-writers of turn-of-the-century America.

Paul Cutright, in *Theodore Roosevelt the Naturalist*, and R.L. Wilson, in *Theodore Roosevelt: Outdoorsman*, offer the necessary background: Roosevelt's boyhood obsession with natural history and shooting, his many writings, his immensely important contributions to resource conservation, his patronage and encouragement of struggling and great naturalists, and so on.[1] Cutright's book tells the story of Roosevelt's work in natural history, but in the train of details it is easy to lose sight of the message that Roosevelt was a genuinely important American naturalist. Moreover, he was regarded as such by many of his peers. Even allowing for the gratitude they felt because he cared so deeply about their work, the opinions of the professional naturalists are still significant.

They were slavish in their praise of him. C. Hart Merriam (for many years chief of the U.S. Biological Survey) recalled, years later, "one evening at my house (where I then had in the neighborhood of five thousand skulls of North American mammals) he astonished everyone— including several eminent naturalists— by picking up skull after skull and mentioning the scientific name of the genus to which it belonged."[2] Earlier, in a paper naming the Olympic elk in honor of Roosevelt, Merriam explained that "it is fitting that the noblest deer of America should perpetuate the name of one who, in the midst of a busy career, has found

I

time to study our larger mammals in their native haunts and has written the best accounts we have ever had of their habits and chase."[3]

It has been claimed by various authorities that Roosevelt's writings (before he became president) about the bighorn sheep, cougar, and grizzly bear were the best published accounts of those species up to that time.[4] Historian Cutright goes further than others on the point, claiming that "none of the large beasts of the West had been treated so completely upon the basis of a single individual's personal knowledge."[5] That may be a little overstated, but we can legitimately place Roosevelt securely among the leading wildlife authorities, in any case. Edmund Heller, a distinguished professional naturalist who accompanied Roosevelt in Africa in 1909–1910, and who later co-authored a book about African animals with him, did not equivocate, claiming for Roosevelt an even broader preeminence:

> The Colonel was a delightful companion, and on our rides afield we had long talks together regarding game animals and zoology generally. He had at his command the entire published literature concerning the game mammals and birds of the world, a feat of memory that few naturalists possess. I felt constantly while with him that I was in the presence of the foremost field naturalist of our time, as indeed I was. His indelible memory seemed to furnish him with all the known facts about any species of game animal, or any phase of vertebrate zoology, or theories concerning it.[6]

For an amateur naturalist to achieve such stature in wildlife science today would not be possible; so great have been the advances in knowledge that it is difficult for a specialist to keep up with current work in just one field, to say nothing of covering the whole subject. Roosevelt became involved in nature study at just about the right time, for though the large western animals had been scientifically described and even studied in captivity, most of what had been written about their natural habits was shallow or unreliable. The only people who had extended contact with big game in the wild (that is, contact of sufficient length to permit observation of the whole life cycle) were hunters, and Roosevelt, with a strong academic background and a broad acquaintance with wildlife literature, knew better than to trust them:

> . . . in spite of popular opinion to the contrary, most old hunters are very untrustworthy in dealing with points of natural

history. They usually know only as much about any given animal as will allow them to kill it.[7]

Some old hunters, even in his day, must be credited with greater reliability than others, and one of Roosevelt's advantages over most of his contemporaries was his keen eye for the believable. He listened to many hunters, mentally checked what they said against the vast reserve of information he had accumulated, and almost always discarded the questionable in favor of the probable. And of all the animals he heard about, of all the animals he hunted, none was the subject of as much questionable reportage as the bear.

If there was a North American game mammal that Roosevelt preferred to hunt over any other, it was probably the elk. To him, the elk was the most majestic member of the deer family, far more attractive than mule deer or white tail deer, far more handsome than the ungainly moose. But the bear excited something in Roosevelt, as it did in many other hunters, that no other North American mammal could match. Bears, particularly grizzlies, were the only truly dangerous American big game. They were the only carnivores pursued by the "still hunt,"[8] and that element of risk gave bear hunting a special appeal to the adventurous hunter.

When Roosevelt first went to the Dakotas in 1883, he had a vague idea that he wanted to hunt the important kinds of game, and maybe become familiar with the land. Within a year he was a rancher, and was involved in a series of extended hunts that would last into the early 1890s. On several of these he was after bear, and though there was probably something of fantasy in the remark, he once wrote to his sister that even in the wild and exhilarating surroundings, full of new experiences, "unless I was bear-hunting all the time I am afraid that I should soon get as restless with this life as with the life at home."[9]

Bears, especially grizzlies, were one important element of what he sought in the West. His quest was one of self-assertion, a devotion to what one historian has called a "cult of manliness." The cult was a matter of pride, of establishing through personal energy and labor one's standing, not just among cowboys or bears, but in society as well.[10] He was out there proving things—to himself, to his family, to his fellow ranchers and cowboys. Much has been written about his successful struggles to improve himself, especially about his efforts to overcome a sickly childhood body. The West provided him with the opportunity to prove himself on a grand scale, in a world of basic, almost elemental, challenges:

> There were all kinds of things of which I was afraid at first, ranging from grizzly bears to "mean" horses to gunfighters; but by acting as if I was not afraid I gradually ceased to be afraid.[11]

This was more than the bravado of a cocky, slightly insecure young man. He chose to test himself as few of his contemporaries would have, even had they felt the need to. Bears were just one unusually colorful and unpredictable part of the test, a part that had the added attraction of being worth writing about.

Roosevelt recognized the magic of the bear, and of its endless appeal to the public mind. He returned to it again and again in his writings, finally amassing a body of information on bears that stands as the finest contribution by a single author to our knowledge of bear habits and hunting prior to the work of William Wright.[12] Roosevelt's many articles on hunting were a mixture of his own observations, his readings, and his carefully sorted fund of information from other sources. He was fortunate enough to hunt with some of the greatest bear hunters of his or any other day; his portrayals of these characters are in themselves an important contribution to bear literature.

His most famous American hunting writings, most of which first appeared in article form, eventually evolved into several books, the most important four of which were *Hunting Trips of a Ranchman* (1885), *Ranch Life and the Hunting Trail* (1888), *The Wilderness Hunter* (1893), and *Outdoor Pastimes of an American Hunter* (1905). These books were enthusiastically greeted by practically all of their reviewers, quite often being placed among the very best of their type.[13] The books have endured, standing as one of the finest contributions by any writer to American hunting literature, and from them come most of the selections in the present volume. Other chapters reprinted here appeared either as articles in periodicals, in later editions of Roosevelt's books, or as chapters in anthologies.

Roosevelt never claimed to be a great hunter, either in the sense of being unusually skilled at stalking and shooting or in the sense of having hunted as much as many of his contemporary "experts" did. In his entire career he certainly killed less than twenty bears, and one need only read his books to see how often he missed shots or committed some clumsy or hilarious gaffe (such as the "clever stalks up to charred logs" described in Chapter Six). He admired the great hunters, and collected and studied their work as few others did, but most of the legend of Roosevelt as a great hunter is just that—a legend. It is an ironic and unjust twist of fate that he is remembered more as a great killer of game than as a great student of wildlife. Had he not become president, it might not have turned out that way.

Roosevelt's Hunting as Historical Scandal

Today, for many reasons and in many circles, Roosevelt's enthusiasm for hunting is held against him. The reasons are not simple, and must be analyzed separately, both in light of actual circumstances (which in some cases have been inaccurately reported) and in the context of Roosevelt's times.

In Roosevelt's day, the term "game hog" was in vogue, and was applied to any hunter or fisherman who killed excessively. Definitions of what constituted an excessive bag varied, but usually one could expect to be criticized if more was killed than could be reasonably used (as in fish that could be eaten before they spoiled) or, more definitely, if one broke some game law or killed so many animals that the sport of others would be diminished.[14] At a time when game laws were just being formulated, and when many species of animals had for many generations been more or less unprotected, it was often difficult to reach a consensus on how much a good sportsman should take.

By the standards of his day, Roosevelt almost never indulged in excessive killing. He was primarily a trophy hunter, killing otherwise only for camp food. Several historians have pointed to what they consider excessive kill totals in his hunting accounts and diaries, but these figures are deceptive and easily misinterpreted. For example, Edmund Morris, in his magnificent *The Rise of Theodore Roosevelt*, quotes at length from an 1884 hunting diary, pointing out that Roosevelt killed "170 items in just forty-seven days."[15] Looking at the diary we see, first, that virtually all were used for camp food. Roosevelt rarely hunted alone, and usually what he shot fed himself and his companions or guide. Next we see that fifty of the "items" were trout, and that a great many more were doves, grouse, ducks, and rabbits. Two hungry, hard-working hunters can consume an enormous quantity of fresh meat in forty-seven days, and it seems unlikely that many of the small game animals were wasted in camp.[16]

Under the circumstances of an extended hunt—some of his were a month or more in duration—there was always a certain amount of waste. Often, unless a permanent camp had been made nearby, hunters could only carry so much meat with them, so they took only the prime portions from an elk or deer, having shot the animal for a trophy in the first place. As well, if they had a choice, most hunters did not eat much bear meat. Some waste occurred, but it was not the sort engendered by blood-thirstiness or what Morris calls "carnage."

Roosevelt's writings reveal that it was a matter of great pride to him that he did not kill excessively. He was extremely self-conscious about good sportsmanship, prone to lecture his readers on it, painfully aware of how many game animals were being slaughtered by thoughtless sport-hunters (though the worst killing of wildlife in his day was by market hunters), and was after all co-founder of one of America's most distinguished sporting fraternities, the Boone and Crockett Club.[17] He practiced what he preached, sometimes giving the impression that he practiced primarily because he dearly enjoyed preaching it afterwards. And there was surely vanity in his rather self-righteous pronouncements that he did not shoot an animal on some occasion because it was not a good enough trophy or because he did not need the meat. But considering the slaughter then going on among wildlife, he was a model of restraint by any reasonable standard.

Another objection to his hunting is often expressed more as bewilderment: how, as one historian put it, "a man who loved animals as much as Roosevelt did could still *enjoy* killing them."[18] There is a point beyond which it is impossible to carry my evaluation of Roosevelt's hunting, and that point is the moral objection many people have to hunting in principle. Here, however, the question is not moral. The above remark is based not on a moral consideration but on an intellectual one; at first glance Roosevelt's desire to kill seems to many to be directly contrary to his well-known affection for wildlife. It seems especially so if one has not read his books or is unfamiliar with the peculiar subculture and elaborate philosophical underpinnings of sport hunting.

Many thousands of pages have been written about sport hunting, quite a few of them devoted to analysis of its rewards. There are a number of provocative and moving testaments to the deep emotional value of hunting. There are, in some cases, ample biological proofs of the *necessity* of cropping certain wildlife populations (though these in no way offer justification for enjoyment of that cropping). There are countless stories that evoke the excitement of the hunt, the thrill of the chase, and the satisfaction of the successful stalk. Hunters generally feel that their experiences bring them very close to the natural world (as do most outdoor recreationists, of course), and that by becoming a part of the life-and-death cycle of a wild animal they appreciate that animal—and value and need its existence as a species—in very special ways. Non-hunters who find Roosevelt's attitude about hunting intellectually unsatisfactory and who want to grasp something of the hunting experience's rewards might be surprised at the depth of the feelings they would encounter in the hunting literature. It may not persuade them to try hunting, and much of it is so poorly written (as is much of the literature of any other outdoor pastime) that it may bore them, but in the best hunting writing there is a sharply expressed awareness of the contradiction of killing something one loves. There is a complex and often misunderstood code of ethics involved in sport hunting at its best, a code that most non-hunters aren't aware of. The historian or layman who passes judgement on Roosevelt's hunting enthusiasm without becoming familiar with hunting's better literature and the philosophy that literature expresses is not doing the sport or Roosevelt justice.

But the intellectual contradiction many see in Roosevelt's hunting can be partly explained in other terms. Roosevelt was a product of a social climate that did not generally disapprove of hunting. He grew up on a steady diet of great natural history books and great adventure and hunting stories. His own hunting library was outstanding. A sickly child, confined for long periods to urban surroundings, he developed a passion for the adventurous life of the frontier, for the wild country so romantically portrayed in the novels of Mayne Reid and Fenimore Cooper. Even in the city, firearms and animals were still a common part of life, and sporting life was a regular outlet for many well-to-do families. As a young man, Roosevelt discovered that he could actually live out his greatest childhood dreams; that he could ride alone across vast prairies, depending only on his sure-footed pony and his rifle. The glamor that a later generation would attach to the cowboy was not yet widespread during his youth. His writings were among the first to solidify (and thereby glamorize) the image of the cowboy as a rustic exemplar of all that's good and true in Americans: hard work, simple justice, and quiet bravery.[19]

He was so enrapt with this western setting that to some extent he romanticized his own involvement in it, an error greatly compounded by those who, in turn, romanticized *him*. David McCullough, in *Mornings on Horseback*, points out that Roosevelt himself was not a cowboy, he was a *ranchman*. Cowboys worked for him, and he with them, but there was a clear social distinction. Roosevelt's proudest western accoutrements were far too expensive for the average cowboy. Roosevelt had his hunting knife custom made at Tiffany's.[20] He was playing at being a western adventurer, writing some eastern rules into the game. The dangers and hardships he faced were no less real for that, but they were somehow less important to his life than they would have been if he had truly gone and lost himself in the West, as some of his more imaginative biographers claimed. Even in his "glory days" of ranching in the Dakotas, the period between 1883 and 1887, when we think of him as living out there, he spent little more than a year actually in western residence. He constantly rode the train between New York and Medora.

This two-sided lifestyle helps to explain the apparent contradiction of Roosevelt as animal lover and animal killer. Roosevelt was not an obsessive killer, or a compulsive hunter. His western adventures were part of an increasingly complicated life, a part that was in most circles acceptable, even admirable. Hunting, as Roosevelt and others of his time pointed out, was a way of keeping fit, of being a good American (of practicing for war, in a sense), and of living a full life.[21] Considering the climate of the times, Roosevelt's behavior was entirely consistent with what might be expected from a well-to-do Victorian gentleman.

But there is yet another aspect of his nature study that fits—intellectually, that is—with his love of hunting. As an important field naturalist ("faunal naturalist," as he put it), Roosevelt was following in the best tradition, a tradition exemplified in the previous generation by the man whose name is more closely linked with nature appreciation than any other in American history, John James Audubon. Audubon was a skilled and enthusiastic wingshot; before high-quality optics and photography, one had to "collect" anything before studying it. Audubon loved hunting, and killed far more birds than he needed for his painting.[22] Similarly, Roosevelt was an avid collector of animal skins even as a child. He was an excellent young taxidermist, and several of his bird mountings are still on exhibit at the American Museum of Natural History. He learned his taxidermy from an old man who, in younger days, had mounted specimens for Audubon. But Roosevelt did not indulge in taxidermy for its own sake: he carefully studied the animals he shot and mounted. Throughout his hunting writings and diaries are references to animal habits; he always recorded the stomach contents of the animals he shot, and such information about feeding habits was hard to come by. If there is need for an intellectual justification for the relatively few bears, or elk, or cougars he killed in his life, it could certainly be found in the quality and quantity of information he was able to pass along because of his hunting.

As well, in a time before national parks and game preserves were common, and before there were ways for the general public to easily appreciate wildlife in its natural setting, it mattered to very few people that many wild animals were being wiped out by habitat destruction and market hunting. Roosevelt was among the first to recognize that hunting, though it killed some animals, could also be the salvation of the greater populations; and that encouraging, especially among young people, good sportsmanship and conservation—by making them right-minded hunters, in other words—was the best way he knew to provide threatened animals with a constituency. Sportsmen were a leading force, perhaps the leading force, in wildlife protection in the late nineteenth century, if only because they were the only group with a vested interest in the welfare of big game.[23] Other types of nature appreciation, such as birdwatching, backpacking, and mountaineering, did not develop politically influential organizations until later, except in some local circumstances.

The least answerable objection to Roosevelt's love of hunting is the moral one; some people believe that sport hunting is beneath proper standards of human conduct. Hunting has been increasingly attacked in recent years as an immoral act. Roosevelt's favorite kind of hunting, trophy hunting, has been most strongly attacked. The taking of the life of an animal for the sheer joy or excitement of the act, or for the pleasure of a household ornament, apalls many people.[24]

Though it is to Roosevelt's benefit in this matter that far fewer people found hunting objectionable in his day than do now, he is also difficult to accuse of immorality. Anyone familiar with his writings knows that he was almost obnoxiously moral—or moralistic—in his thinking. At some point or another, he used all of his books as pulpits. He seems to modern readers to have been self-righteous at times (the moral snobbery in his college diaries is almost laughable today). He had very strong notions of what constituted proper moral conduct, and those notions pervade his hunting writing.

Good sportsmanship was most important of all, but he carried his judgements on the outdoor life beyond that. He condemned, for example, anyone for whom sport itself became a way of life. He applauded the hunters who took the trouble to study the habits of game, thereby contributing to scientific knowledge. The chapters that follow show many instances of Roosevelt pinning down a simple hunting activity and turning it into a moral issue. Of course he commonly criticized hunters who used illegal means of killing animals, or behaved in any ungentlemanly fashion. If by some people's standards today (or even in his own time), hunting is morally unjustifiable, Roosevelt's pursuit of that sport was not the result of a lack of a firm moral code; it was instead the result of the presence of a different moral code.

Roosevelt's hunting became a particularly sensitive issue once he was a well-known political figure. He was naturally the target of many kinds of criticisms, some of which were generated by good impulse, others that were prompted solely by political animosity, and yet others that resulted from some combination of the two. Once he was president his every action was subjected to intense scrutiny, commentaries on many levels, and the usual assortment of journalistic adventuring.[25]

One or two of his hunts became fiascoes despite his efforts to restrict the number of press representatives, local officials, and assorted hangers-on who found their way into camp. More than one hunt was hurt or ruined by this problem, which brought up a worse situation for Roosevelt. As president, given the public (both national and international) exposure his hunts received, he could almost not afford an unsuccessful hunt. Beyond the simple embarrassment of failure (though Roosevelt knew as well as any hunter that you don't always get the game) was the delight his political opponents would take in it. It did not reflect well on the office, either, for the president to fail at something so consumately manly as a bear hunt.

Roosevelt became particularly sensitive about the public reception of his hunting after the worst hunt of his life—an unsuccessful bear hunt that, ironically, forever linked his name to the elusive prey.

In November of 1902 Roosevelt went on a six-day bear hunt near Smedes, Mississippi. One of his more presidential reasons for being in the area was a touchy political situation involving racial equality, but the hunt was purely a vacation. He was the guest of various prominent local citizens, and the hunt did not go well. Finally, after several unsuccessful days, a bedraggled black bear of about 230 pounds was run down by the dogs and securely roped. The president, hunting elsewhere at the time, was summoned to kill the bear, but he indignantly refused to shoot the bear under such unsporting conditions. He told his guide to have the animal killed, practicing his own past sermons about the difference between sport and simple killing.[26]

Within hours the story was out (that was the only bear Roosevelt got close to on the trip). Several cartoons appeared showing Roosevelt with the bear (a small cub in the cartoons), the most famous of which were produced by Clifford Berryman of the *Washington Post*. These were entitled "Drawing the Line in Mississippi," a double *entendre* involving both Roosevelt's drawing the line between good sportsmanship and bad, and Roosevelt's involvement with the racial issue—the "color line," as it was called.[27]

Morris Michtom, a Russian-Jewish immigrant in Brooklyn, was inspired by the cartoon to create a small toy bear for that Christmas season. He called it "Teddy's Bear," and allegedly wrote the president for permission to use his name. The correspondence has not survived, but the story is told that Roosevelt replied with bemusement, "I don't think my name will mean much to the bear business, but you're welcome to use it."[28] Of course it turned out that the name *did* mean much; within a year the sale of Teddy Bears was so good that Michtom formed a new, larger company under the name of the Ideal Toy Company, now a giant in the toy industry, and the Teddy Bear became a great American (and international) toy.[29]

Roosevelt seems never to have spoken publicly about the Teddy Bear, or at least he never gave the matter much attention. He also seems to have ignored another bear-related item, a series of cartoon adventures that appeared in twenty newspapers (including the *New York Times*) about "The Roosevelt Bears." These two adult bears were depicted in various travels (Chicago, Boston, Niagara Falls) by cartoonists V.F. Campbell and R.K. Culver, with text by Seymour Eaton. Later, the cartoons were republished in book form (it has recently been reprinted). Like the original Teddy Bear cartoon and its toy namesake, they helped fix the bear in the public mind as a symbol for Roosevelt. Some other cartoonists later used the·bear, usually a small cub, as a character in Roosevelt-related cartoons, but Roosevelt apparently never considered the animal a personal symbol, preferring the much less popular moose.[30]

He was, however, troubled by the bad publicity his hunt had received. Shortly after the hunt, writing to a western friend, Philip Stewart, about a hunt he was considering making in Colorado, he gave his version of the story:

> I have just had a most unsatisfactory experience in a bear hunt in Mississippi. There were plenty of bears, and if I had gone alone or with one companion I would have gotten one or two. But my kind hosts, with best of intentions, insisted upon turning the affair into a cross between a hunt and a picnic, which always results in a failure for the hunt and usually in a failure for the picnic. On this occasion, as a picnic it was pleasant enough, but as a hunt simply exasperating, and I never got a shot. Naturally the comic press jumped at the failure and have done a good deal of laughing over it.
>
> I mention all this because the amount of trouble I had in connection therewith has made me hesitate about our hunt. As it was, I had to compromise on taking three thoroughly reputable newspapermen to the station from which I got off and letting them occasionally come out to visit the camp; and even under these circumstances it was literally only by the use of guards armed with

shotguns that I prevented the yellow journal men from coming along too . . .

I am really at a loss to make up my mind whether it would be possible to take a hunt without having people join us in a way that will interfere with the hunting and without having so much silly and brutal newspaper talk as to leave an unpleasant impression upon the immense number of our people who know nothing whatever of hunting and who accept as true what they see in the press.[31]

His bitterness was more than personal embarrassment; the year before, during a hunt in Colorado when he was vice president-elect, Roosevelt had managed to separate himself from the press, leaving them with no choice, in their minds at least, but to fabricate incredible stories. The *New York Herald,* accepting every imaginary word sent it by its bored reporter, claimed that in a few days hunting Roosevelt killed 303 assorted creatures, including 46 lions.[32] The newspaper claimed that he was attacked by wolves, chased by a grizzly, and ran down a huge mountain lion after an eight-mile run in a four-horse tally-ho. Roosevelt had plenty of reason to mistrust the press.

Following the debacle in Mississippi, Roosevelt hesitated to announce his next bear hunt. In planning the second trip to Colorado, for example, he made it known that he was after cougar, though in truth he also wanted bear. He decided to keep quiet about the bears, and said as much to Philip Stewart:

I cannot afford to make a failure of this hunt if I go. I should not say anything about the bears. I should simply say that we are going for mountain lions, because with Goff's pack [of dogs] we are certain to get a mountain lion if we can start one.[33]

Roosevelt recognized that his sport was no longer his own, and that appearances mattered more than they ever had before.

He was not speaking egotistically when he said that the public does not understand the hunt. Any outdoor enthusiast, whether birdwatcher, fisherman, or hang-glider, knows the sting of ignorant ridicule. In Roosevelt's case a good example would be hunting with dogs, as he did in Mississippi, and later in Colorado and Louisiana. When used, dogs become a very important part of the sport; the chase, with the gradually intensifying clamor of the hounds, is the heart of the experience, just the way it is in the more formal fox hunt. And, as in fox hunting, there might be many hunters, all "in on the kill," which is to say that the Mississippi hunt, had it been composed of a normal group of hunters, could have been a success in sporting terms even if some of the hunters did not themselves actually kill a bear. Roosevelt's point was that such subtleties were lost on the public, and he was right.

Public concern, most often expressed by animal-lovers (though also expressed by people concerned for Roosevelt's safety), was voiced frequently. When he announced plans for his 1903 visit to Yellowstone Park, and invited the famous old Catskill naturalist John Burroughs to accompany him, a woman from Vermont wrote to Burroughs about the President's hunting. According to Burroughs, who was known as a passive and gentle soul, she wanted him to "teach the President to love the animals as much as I did, as if he did not love them much more, because his love is founded upon knowledge, and because they had been a part of his life."[34] The animals at issue in this case were cougars, which at that time were often shot by soldiers in the park; it was thought that the cougars were harming the herds of elk and deer in the park, and Roosevelt's inquiry to the park's superintendent about the possibility of hunting the cougars with the soldiers had gotten out.[35] Roosevelt found it wise to announce he would do no hunting in the park, but Burroughs, a worshipful admirer, remained outspoken about the president's right to hunt big game. In contrast to Burroughs, later on that same trip Roosevelt spent some time in Yosemite Park in California with John Muir, who chided him for his "boyish" habit of killing things.

Roosevelt faced this public attention the rest of his life. When he was planning his trip to Africa at the close of his second term, the New Hampshire Women's Humane Society asked him to give up the hunt because "the force of his example will tend to increase the slaughter of animals for the sake of sport."[36]

Of course some of the criticism he received was not motivated by humanitarian concern. Much of it resulted from personal or political animosity. Roosevelt had some eloquent critics, perhaps none more so than Mark Twain, who commented in his diaries on Roosevelt's successful Louisiana hunt in 1907. Though these remarks were not published at the time, they exemplify the high comedy some of Roosevelt's critics saw in presidential hunts. Twain entitled his remarks "The Hunting of the Cow."

> Two colossal historical incidents took place yesterday, incidents which can never be forgotten while histories continue to be written. Yesterday, for the first time, business was opened to

commerce by the Marconi Company and wireless messages sent entirely across the Atlantic, straight from shore to shore; on that same day the President of the United States for the fourteenth time came within three miles of flushing a bear. As usual he was far away, nobody knew where, when the bear burst upon the multitude of dogs and hunters and equerries and chamberlains in waiting, and sutlers and cooks and scullions, and Rough Riders and infantry and artillery, and had his customary swim to the other side of the pond and disappeared in the woods. While half the multitude watched the place where he had vanished the other half galloped off, with horns blowing, to scour the state of Louisiana in search of the great hunter. Why don't they stop hunting the bear altogether and hunt the President? He is the only one of the pair that can't be found when he is wanted.[37]

And later, when Roosevelt (who was upset at his oversized entourage, knowing that a small party would have had much better hunting) finally got his bear, Twain exclaimed,

> Alas, the President has got that cow after all. If it was a cow. Some say it was a bear—a real bear. These were eyewitnesses, but they were all White House domestics; they are all under wages to the great hunter, and when a witness is in that condition it makes his testimony doubtful. The fact that the President himself thinks it was a bear does not diminish the doubt but enlarges it.[38]

All this attention had little effect on Roosevelt's personal hunting philosophy. After he became president he found it easier to channel most of his trophies to appropriate scientific institutions (where they were genuinely needed and appreciated), and he frequently referred to his hunting in terms of its ancillary worth as specimen collecting. His great adventure in Africa, originally planned as a private expedition, took on new meaning for him and the public when the Smithsonian Institution agreed to send along a staff of scientists to preserve his trophies for their collection. His safari was fabulously successful in terms of providing the National Museum with a good African collection, and he proudly reported, at the conclusion of his book *African Game Trails*, that he and his son Kermit "kept about a dozen trophies for ourselves; otherwise we shot nothing that was not used either as a museum specimen or for meat— usually for both purposes." He seems never to have wavered from his conviction that hunting, whether for meat or sport, was not only morally acceptable but also morally important:

There is no need to exercise much patience with men who protest against field sports, unless, indeed, they are logical vegetarians of the flabbiest Hindoo type. If no deer or rabbits were killed, no crops could be cultivated. If it is morally right to kill an animal to eat its body, then it is morally right to kill it to preserve its head. A good sportsman will not hesitate as to the relative value he puts upon the two, and to get the one he will go a long time without eating the other. No nation facing the unhealthy softening and relaxation of fibre which tend to accompany civilization can afford to neglect anything that will develop hardihood, resolution, and the scorn of discomfort and danger.

"But," he concluded, "if sport is made an end instead of a means, it is better to avoid it altogether."[39]

Bear Study in Roosevelt's Time

During the nineteenth century, human attitudes toward animals changed considerably. Because of the great technological advances brought about by the Industrial Revolution, the average person became relatively distant from animals compared to earlier times, often depending directly upon no visible beasts of burden in the course of daily life. Once people were able to view the "lower forms" of life from a comfortable distance, and once they were no longer dependent upon animal labor, they could afford the luxury of compassion for the condition of animals in the world. At the same time, the spread of Darwin's theories—part of a general scientific awakening that had actually begun in the previous century—brought dumb animals into a new perspective and also made humans reconsider their own animal nature. The upshot of Darwinism was often an increased feeling of kinship with other animals, and a greater concern for their well-being.[40]

The rise of the scientific method and of the modern university system gave new discipline and depth to the study of those same animals. By 1800, even many laymen were uncomfortable with the hodgepodge of myth, superstition, and casual observation that passed for natural history, and the following hundred years saw the establishment of much better ways for dealing with questions of natural history.

The literature of bears is an excellent example of the gradual sophistication of nature study. In Topsell's *The History of Four-Footed Beasts* (1607) we are treated to an exposition of nature as miracle: his bears kidnapped and seduced maids, nursed abandoned human infants, putrified fresh meat by breathing on it, and copulated for weeks at a time (they "disjoin not themselves again until they be made lean"). Mixed with such wondrous information was a fair amount of error of a more practical sort: that bears had very thin skulls and were most easily killed "by a small blow on his head," or that "they are very hardly tamed." But far more important, even at this early date, is the assortment of sound or somehow defensible information. Perhaps it only seems important because of its apposition to so many fables, but from Topsell and his contemporaries we learn, among many other things, that bears hibernate ("choosing rather to suffer famine than cold; lying for the most part three or four months together and never see the light, whereby their guts grow so empty, that they are almost closed up and stick together"), that they give birth to extraordinarily small young ("no bigger than rats"), that they bury their dead (not true in itself, but probably based on the now well-established habit that grizzly bears share with some other predators, that of performing token burials of carrion), and that they rarely attack someone who plays dead (playing dead is now the most frequently recommended way to avoid being attacked by a bear one has surprised at close quarters).[41]

From this fantasy world, where folklore and direct observation were given equal credence, it was a long and halting climb to the modern scientific perspective, and even today—and far more so in Roosevelt's time—the bear has not been freed from all of its myths.

We can best follow the progress of bear study, and thereby appreciate Roosevelt's knowledge, by examining a few specific aspects of bear life. Probably the most mysterious and remarked-upon trait of bears has been hibernation. Bears, except in extreme southern latitudes, commonly den up for three to six months, during which time they pass no food or liquid through their systems.[42] Most other mammalian hibernators actually come out of their stupor periodically to eat previously stored foods (or go find such foods), urinate, and defecate. Bears simply drop into a deep sleep and stay there for the duration. Hibernation is something we've heard about all our lives; we see it in cartoons and story books as children, and by the time we grow up we aren't impressed by it any more. In human terms, hibernation is the equivalent of eating a big Thanksgiving dinner and then sleeping until Easter. Nature writers of the seventeenth and eighteenth centuries were not dulled to the wonder of it; some of them didn't even believe it was possible:

> It is credibly asserted that they have been kept chained up
> all the winter without anything to eat or drink, and that when it

was ended they continued very fat; but every one is left to his own liberty to believe what he pleases in this respect; for it is certainly very strange, that an animal so well provided with fur should be so extremely unwilling to stir abroad in the winter time.[43]

Hibernation is not so much a response to extreme cold as to a seasonal shortage of food. The bear's warm coat is as necessary to it in the den as it would be outside. Even a century later, long after many bears had been observed through winters in zoos, an American writer asserted that it seemed "highly improbable" that bears could den up for several months without eating.[44] By the early 1880s, though, it was generally conceded that they did just that. How they got along without food remained unclear. A few American authors sustained Topsell's belief that bears survived by sucking sustenance from their forepaws.[45] The more objective and critical observers understood, however, that bears did indeed hibernate, "for the most part in a state of lethargy, abstaining altogether from food, and subsisting upon the absorption of the fat which he has accumulated in the course of the summer."[46]

A separation occurred during the nineteenth century that further complicated the progress of bear study. As a true scientific literature grew, its growth was accompanied by the continuation of a popular literature, the latter expanding rapidly as advances in printing technology permitted the rapid expansion of periodical literature. The specialization of biologists was often lost on the general public, so that by the late 1880s, though scientists had accumulated an impressive amount of information about nature, much of it hadn't filtered down to the public. (The same situation holds true today; one can read dozens of bear stories in outdoor magazines and never learn from them that thousands of pages of accurate natural history information are in print elsewhere.) This has a bearing on any evaluation of Roosevelt's bear writings because one of his strong suits was his acquaintance with scientific literature, and another was his discerning eye—his ability to sift questionable information.

A good example of this growing gap between scientific and popular knowledge of bears involved the mating season. Though by Roosevelt's time scientists had determined that bears mate in early summer, many popular writers and hunters still believed that mating occurred shortly before hibernation.[47]

There were other common fallacies about bears, some of which endure even today. One of the most popular—and at once frightening and endearing—is the bear hug. It is often claimed that bears kill their prey by hugging it to death. In the 1890s Roosevelt was one of a few people willing to question this notion, but now it has fallen completely out of fashion. It probably resulted from observations of bears wrapping their forelegs around some animal or person to hold it still while biting it.

An unusually complex issue of great interest to nineteenth century hunters, and of even greater interest to modern bear managers, was the matter of aggressiveness. When white men first began to encounter grizzly bears regularly, about the time of Lewis and Clark, the grizzly was said to be very "ferocious," almost always attacking on sight, and very hard to kill. At the beginning of the 1800s, firearms were still fairly primitive, one-shot affairs, capable of deadly accuracy but not especially powerful. As the century passed, more modern weapons were developed and bears became much easier to kill. Even today, however, the grizzly or even the black bear, because of great strength and heavy skull and frame, can "take a lot of killing," as the old hunters used to say.[48]

Most hunters claimed (and still do) that the grizzly changed as firearms became more effective. They believed that the bears, as a species, learned that they were not a match for firearms, and that the bears therefore chose to be less belligerent when encountering humans. The standard story, as told by Roosevelt and others, was that the late nineteenth-century grizzly bear would probably flee at the sight of men.

It is difficult, however, to tell how many of the grizzlies encountered by early trappers and explorers charged "at first sight," because in those cases where details are given it becomes evident that the men were often the aggressors. In many cases, the attacking bears were sows with young, possibly feeling threatened. In many other cases, the bear's "first sight" came after the men had put a few bullets into it from ambush. We probably don't have enough good evidence to make many generalizations about grizzly bear behavior before 1860, but even if we had more information we would be plagued by countless variables. It could be, for example, that the grizzlies early travelers encountered in open terrain—that is, grizzlies who followed the buffalo herds—were quite aggressive; there is good biological reason for a bear in open country to develop greater aggressive tendencies than a bear in the forest might need.[49] Open-country grizzlies were all but gone once the bison were destroyed, leaving grizzlies in more forested, rugged country to provide the encounters had by men in the late 1800s. It could be that, over eighty years or so of hunting, men actually did cull from most grizzly populations the aggressive individuals, the way fishermen might harvest the stupidest (or most easily caught) trout from each generation of fish and inadvertently produce a less catchable race of fish. These questions are hardly academic today, as managers of wilderness areas and national parks try to understand as much as possible how wild bears respond to people; many theories have been offered. Some say, for example, that occasional hunting would keep bears from getting too bold around people. Others point out that bears in national parks, such as Yellowstone and Glacier, generally flee if they hear people coming from some distance off, and that hunting–illegal in national parks anyway–could disrupt normal population distribution. It is all very complicated, more so than Roosevelt ever would have imagined. And, whatever the actual situation might have been, grizzlies still did attack people–usually hunters–in Roosevelt's day, just as they do today. The grizzly, in any age, is an unpredictable animal, each individual having a distinct personality and being subject to the normal range of influences that direct its actions.

Another aspect of human contact with bears was that many writers believed that bears became nocturnal where they were hunted. This is entirely possible (though some bears are nocturnal under natural circumstances anyway), bears being remarkably adjustable animals. A good, if somewhat disheartening, example is the national park black bear. Until recently in a number of national parks black bears often spent large parts of the day parked along the roads gathering in dill pickles and ice cubes from passing cars. Once the bears realized the profitability of begging, they altered not only their movement habits but their daily schedules to accommodate the traffic, just as other bears adjusted theirs to accommodate the garbage trucks at park dumps. The extent to which such adjustments are made, and the extent to which the bears can readjust to non-garbage feeding conditions, have been important and hotly-argued issues in park management circles in recent years.[50]

Though there did exist a formidable knowledge of bears by the time Roosevelt started writing, it was scattered widely through a poorly organized and often obscure periodical literature. Most of it was not available to the public. And though a concerted effort was being made to study many forms of wildlife at that time, the bears were pretty much left out of the picture. They were victims of unusual social and scientific circumstances.

As far as the public was concerned, the bear had little redeeming social value outside of fairy tales. In many circles it was not the esteemed aesthetic object that deer or elk were (deer and elk being, of course, "harmless"). It was often treated like a varmint.[51] Though it became a game animal in some states, such protection usually occurred after the animal was mostly extirpated or its range disastrously reduced.[52] Hunters sought it, but not frequently (or successfully) enough to have a major interest in its welfare–at least nowhere near the interest they showed in deer. Deer and other ungulates were the major targets of American big game hunters. Bears, being far less numerous under normal circumstances than deer, were not able to generate an influential following among hunters. As true as this was of black bears, it was even more decisively true of grizzlies. Western ranchers and settlers quickly realized that the grizzly was not as tractable as the black bear, and could not be tolerated. In 1800 the grizzly ranged widely over the western half of North America. Even by Roosevelt's time, as he reported, their range was greatly reduced, and today there are less than 1,000 remaining in the lower forty-eight states, almost all of them being confined to a few wilderness areas and national parks in Idaho, Montana, and Wyoming.[53]

In late nineteenth century scientific circles, fate dealt the grizzly bear a peculiar and still not well understood blow that probably retarded public appreciation of bears even further. It happened, ironically, because bears came to the attention of one of America's foremost wildlife scientists, Clinton Hart Merriam.

C. Hart Merriam was chief of the Bureau of Biological Survey (Department of Agriculture) from 1885 to 1910. In his career he produced hundreds of articles, pamphlets, and reports on various biological subjects. He was fabulously prolific. Bears attracted his attention early in his tenure as chief of the Bureau, and it quickly became known that Merriam was involved in an exhaustive study of the speciation and natural history of North American bears, especially grizzlies. Writing in 1955, biologists Tracey Storer and Lloyd Tevis, Jr., suggested that Merriam's interest in bears probably kept others from studying them. His preeminence in the scientific world probably would have discouraged most of his colleagues.[54]

Unfortunately, Merriam's great research was of little use to the public. In fact, it was of little use to science, and therein lies an issue which involved Roosevelt in a rare head-on confrontation with the great scientist.

Merriam's great preoccupation was species description. He was what was, and is, known as a splitter: a scientist who tends to break a group of animals down into smaller and smaller, and ever more subtly distinct, species. Working with his wonderful collection of grizzly skulls, and constantly gathering more of them from all over North America, he began to describe new species of grizzly bears, basing his work on variations in skull shape and proportions. In 1896 his total was over thirty species. By 1918 he believed there were eighty-six species of grizzly bears in North America.[55]

The traditional mode of establishing an animal as a distinct species hinges on its breeding habits; if it does not interbreed with another animal (that is, if interbreeding is impossible or produces only sterile offspring, like the mule), it is generally considered a separate species from that animal. Many of Merriam's supposed species did interbreed – some may even have been sibling cubs from the same litter. In his broad work with North American mammals (he was also splitting coyotes, wolves, and others), Merriam was causing great confusion among scientists. He was a leader in the field, and yet he was not following accepted procedures. In Roosevelt's time, even in the 1910s, Merriam seemed to hold sway despite the inadequacies of his approach.

The story of Roosevelt's encounter with Merriam is told by Paul Cutright in *Theodore Roosevelt the Naturalist*.[56] For our purposes it is enough to say that Roosevelt, though he had an admirable command of such matters as skull variation, was convinced that what Merriam considered species distinctions were no more significant than variations between individuals of one species, the way human heads vary in size and shape. Roosevelt got involved fairly early in Merriam's work. In a famous article in *Science* in April of 1897, he expressed his disagreement both humbly (admitting he was a layman, and not really qualified to argue) and strongly.[57] Later that year he was invited to present his case to the Biological Society of Washington. His long speech was apparently well-received, but just as apparently not a success. The reporter on the scene concluded that though many present were extremely impressed with Roosevelt's grasp of the issues, Merriam's short rebuttal "completely demolished the Rooseveltian argument."[58]

It would be interesting to know what Merriam said, considering that in the long run, despite Merriam's continued work and the 1918 publication of his "Review of the Grizzly and Brown Bears of North America," Roosevelt was proven right.[59] Eventually practically all of Merriam's splitting was undone. Roosevelt's simpler, more practical approach won out. As he stated at the time, "I may as well confess that I have certain conservative instincts which are jarred when an old familiar friend is suddenly cut up into eleven brand new acquaintances."[60]

The ultimate failure of Merriam's approach to take hold was only a part of the bad news for bears. Merriam was at work on a book about bears, one he never completed (the manuscript may survive). He was not a popularizer, and was happy enough producing a steady flow of pamphlets and technical papers read only within the scientific community. Again, Roosevelt respectfully differed with him, repeatedly encouraging him to write up his work in a great book of wildlife natural history. It did not happen. Merriam, by dominating bear science for thirty or more years, and by not producing anything popularly palatable, may have greatly retarded public appreciation of bears. The public had to pick up what it could from the unreliable popular periodicals, or go to fictionalized accounts such as Seton's *The Biography of a Grizzly* (1899) and *Monarch the Big Bear of Tallac* (1904) until William Wright's books *The Grizzly Bear* and *Ben, The Black Bear* were published in 1909, followed a decade later by the less reliable *The Grizzly* by Enos Mills. Other popular bear books followed those, but another half century would pass before a bonafide bear scientist would provide the public with a popular volume on bears.

In the meantime, readers would turn to other sources, and among the most prominent were the writings of Theodore Roosevelt.

Roosevelt's Bear Writings in Perspective

Roosevelt's writings are not presented here as a polished treatise that will cover, evenly and uniformly, all aspects of bear hunting and natural history. He wrote this material for a variety of publications over a twenty-eight-year period, learning much along the way. There are a few inconsistencies, such as instances where he disagrees with something he said earlier, but they aren't bothersome, and they don't detract from the story he tells in any important way.

His natural history, with few exceptions, was as reliable as could be had at the time. He had a healthy suspicion for reports of bears of great weight,[61] he understood the basic elements of bear diet, he knew their denning habits, and he knew their daily routine. His hunting descriptions and advice were equally sound.

But he had some things wrong. In matters of mating and cub-rearing, he was not so much incorrect as vague. He wrote very little about the mating habits of either black or grizzly bear, though he surely was familiar with contemporary literature on the subject. His material on the grizzly bear in Chapter Two has been called the most "thorough and satisfactory" account of the "private life of the grizzly" that had been written to that date.[62] It probably was; at least I am unaware of any other single account that equalled it. In it there is one brief paragraph about the mating season that, though it accurately describes the battles between boars for the sows, does not say when mating takes place. We can probably assume that Roosevelt knew more than he wrote, but considering the confusion on that subject at the time it is a little surprising that he didn't comment on it. His familiarity with family life is evident because he was ahead of his time in pointing out that sow bears, whose fierce defense of their young is legend, will sometimes desert young if threatened.[63] On the other hand, he mistakenly assumed that grizzly sows, like black bear sows, always separate from their young in the fall of the cub's first year. Recent research has shown that many grizzly cubs are weaned as two-and-a-half-year-olds, and some stay with the mother even longer.[64]

Roosevelt the hunter was especially interested in bear behavior and "temperament."[65] For him and his sporting colleagues, temperament meant mostly "how does it react when hunted or shot?" Generally his impressions on bear behavior were very good, though, as mentioned earlier, he shared the common belief that grizzlies had radically altered their behavior during the nineteenth century—an opinion now less widely held. He was also aware that some charges made by bears are really only bluffs (others being nothing more than a bear running up to get a closer look at the chargee), that bears do not advance to attack on two feet (as in modern movies), and that hugging is not done to crush the victim.[66]

In one embarrassing instance his research seems to have failed him badly. He didn't understand the origins of the name of the grizzly bear. Earliest reports of the grizzly to reach eastern North America came from trappers and traders in Canada who told of a large bear with a "grizzled" coat, that is a coat of mixed color, usually brown and gray. By the time of Lewis and Clark, the term "grizzle" or grizzly had begun to acquire its second meaning, that of a bear with a grisly disposition.[67] In his writings Roosevelt switched back and forth between grizzly and grisly, maintaining rather dejectedly that though grisly was correct, grizzly appeared to be winning out. By about 1900 he seems to have resigned himself to spelling it in the now-accepted form.

But the gaps in Roosevelt's knowledge were gaps in the greater knowledge of the time. One of the values, and certainly one of the pleasures, of his outdoor writing is the feeling the reader gets of the learning process that was going on. When Roosevelt editorialized against unsportsmanlike conduct as he defined it, or about bear behavior, or about the controversy over splitting bears into more species, he was participating in an important dialogue, the result of which was no less than the evolution of current bear science and the equally important evolution of the code of sporting ethics bears deserved. In his preachings about good sport and natural history, he encouraged his audience to a higher appreciation of both.

A NOTE ON THE SELECTIONS

The process of tracing the origins of these writings was a fascinating lesson in Roosevelt's literary economy. He rarely wasted periodical material; most of what he wrote for periodical publication found its way into a book eventually. It was interesting to watch the passage of these writings from first to final form.

The following chapters are not arranged in strict chronological order. I have attempted to place first those chapters that concentrate most heavily on bear natural history and behavior. This is only the most general sort of organization, of course, because in Roosevelt's writings hunting and natural history were part of the same process; one succeeded at hunting because one understood natural history, and one appreciated natural history because one hunted. The first nine chapters were the result of his western experiences in the 1880s and 1890s. The last three involve trips made during his presidency. I have presented the chapters here as they appeared in Roosevelt's books, assuming that this was the way he wanted them to last (many were slightly edited, either by him or by the publisher, so that their earlier, article form is different from their book form). In the case of the final chapter, on Louisiana, I have presented the article form because this story was not included in any of his books until after his death.

Where possible I have retained his titles, but some short selections (Chapters Five and Ten) required titling. Chapter Nine, "A Mysterious Enemy," had its final form as part of a longer chapter in *The Wilderness Hunter,* and so I used the title that it had when it first appeared in *The Youth's Companion* on August 31, 1893. Chapter Three, "The Bear's Disposition," first appeared as part of a Boone and Crockett Club book in 1897. Roosevelt dropped it into the narrative of his Colorado bear hunt (Chapter Eleven), from which I have deleted it, believing that it stands better on its own.

In the appendix to *The Wilderness Hunter*, Roosevelt pointed out that he had "avoided repeating what was contained in either of my former books, the *Hunting Trips of a Ranchman* and *Ranch Life and the Hunting Trail.*" That is generally true, but the careful reader will recognize some incidents that Roosevelt retold in different ways to make different points. He might have recalled an event in more than one book, but it was usually to illustrate a point not previously made.

It is important to keep in mind that these selections were written many years ago, and that our knowledge of wildlife has improved immensely since then. Though, as I have stated, most of Roosevelt's natural history is reliable, this book is not published as an authoritative, up-to-date guide to bears. In many particulars, such as current status of bear populations in various parts of the country, Roosevelt's accounts are unreliable. (Enos Mills's book *The Grizzly* [1919] was recently republished with the announcement on its cover that it is "the classic study" of the grizzly bear, something it wasn't even in 1919.) This book of Roosevelt's bear writings is not presented as replacement for many excellent scientific reports now available. Bear science has reached a point that Roosevelt didn't even dream of, and I recommend the modern scientific literature to readers who want to learn more. A number of papers and reports are mentioned in the notes to the Introduction.

Roosevelt would probably be gratified to learn how well some of the big game animals of North America have fared since he died. The deer, elk, and pronghorn are far better off than they were when he was writing. Even the bison, though not really a game animal these days, has recovered from near extinction to secure numbers. Others, such as the bighorn and the mountain goat, are not doing as well. As for the bears, the black bear continues to demonstrate enough flexibility to survive in healthy numbers in many parts of the United States; in parts of New England it is better off than at any time since the early 1800s. But for the grizzly, Roosevelt's "chief of American game," the future is clouded with uncertainty. The flood of settlement and development that Roosevelt predicted in 1885 has reduced the grizzly bear to a few scattered populations whose ranges are being whittled away by the alarming variety of pressures we dignify with such names as society, civilization, and, worst of all, progress. The final extermination of the grizzly bear from the lower forty-eight states is approaching fast. Unless we do something about it now, right away, it will most surely happen. When it does, we will have lost something immeasurably precious, something that could have been preserved through only a little moderation and good sense.

A Note on the Selections

Sources of the Readings

The Black Bear." *The Wilderness Hunter* (New York: G.P. Putnam's Sons, 1893), pp. 255–64.

"Old Ephraim, The Grisly Bear." *The Wilderness Hunter*, pp. 265–95.

"The Bear's Disposition." *Trail and Campfire* (New York: Forest and Stream Publishing Company, 1897), pp. 230–37.

"A Cattle-Killing Bear." *Good Hunting* (New York: Harper and Brothers Publishers, 1907), pp. 27–37.

"A Black Bear Hunt in the Selkirks." *The Wilderness Hunter*, pp. 136–39.

"Old Ephraim." *Hunting Trips of a Ranchman* (New York: G.P. Putnam's Sons, 1885), pp. 140–86.

"Hunting the Grizzly." *The Wilderness Hunter*, pp. 296–334.

"A Man-Killing Bear." *The Youth's Companion*, July 13, 1893, p. 354.

"A Mysterious Enemy." *The Wilderness Hunter*, pp. 441–47.

"Bears in the Yellowstone." *Outdoor Pastimes of an American Hunter* (New York: Charles Scribner's Sons, 1905), pp. 347–51.

"A Colorado Bear Hunt." *Outdoor Pastimes of an American Hunter*, pp. 76–111.

"In the Louisiana Canebreaks." *Scribner's Magazine*, January, 1908, pp. 47–60.

AMERICAN BEARS

The engraved frontispiece to *Hunting Trips of a Ranchman*, derived from an 1885 studio photograph of Roosevelt. Courtesy of the Theodore Roosevelt Collection, Harvard College Library.

The
Black Bear
Chapter I

Next to the whitetail deer the black bear is the commonest and most widely distributed of American big game. It is still found quite plentifully in northern New England, in the Adirondacks, Catskills, and along the entire length of the Alleghanies, as well as in the swamps and canebreaks of the southern states. It is also common in the great forests of northern Michigan, Wisconsin, and Minnesota, and throughout the Rocky Mountains and the timbered ranges of the Pacific coast. In the East it has always ranked second only to the deer among the beasts of chase. The bear and the buck were the staple objects of pursuit of all the old hunters. They were more plentiful than the bison and elk even in the long vanished days when these two great monarchs of the forest still ranged eastward to Virginia and Pennsylvania. The wolf and the cougar were always too scarce and too shy to yield much profit to the hunter. The black bear is a timid, cowardly animal, and usually a vegetarian, though it sometimes preys on the sheep, hogs, and even cattle of the settler, and is very fond of raiding his corn and melons. Its meat is good and its fur often valuable; and in its chase there is much excitement, and occasionally a slight spice of danger, just enough to render it attractive; so it has always been eagerly followed. Yet it still holds its own, though in greatly diminished numbers, in the more thinly settled portions of the country. One of the standing riddles of American zoology is the fact that the black bear, which is easier killed and less prolific than the wolf, should hold its own in the land better than the latter, this being directly the reverse of what occurs in Europe, where the brown bear is generally exterminated before the wolf.

In a few wild spots in the East, in northern Maine for instance, here and there in the neighborhood of the upper Great Lakes, in the east Tennessee and Kentucky mountains and the swamps of Florida and Mississippi, there still lingers an occasional representative of the old wilderness hunters. These men live in log-cabins in the wilderness. They do their hunting on foot, occasionally with the help of a single trailing dog. In Maine they are as apt to kill moose and caribou as bear and deer; but elsewhere the two last, with an occasional cougar or wolf, are the beasts of chase which they follow. Nowadays as these old hunters die there is no one to take their places, though there are still plenty of backwoods settlers in all of the regions named who do a great deal of hunting and trapping. Such an old hunter rarely makes his appearance at the settlements except to dispose of his peltry and hides in exchange for cartridges and provisions, and he leads a life of such lonely isolation as to insure his individual characteristics developing into peculiarities. Most of the wilder districts in the eastern states still preserve memories of some such old hunter who lived his long life alone, waging ceaseless warfare on the vanishing game, whose oddities, as well as his courage, hardihood, and woodcraft, are laughingly remembered by the older settlers, and who is usually best known as having killed the last wolf or bear or cougar ever seen in the locality.

Generally the weapon mainly relied on by these old hunters is the rifle; and occasionally some old hunter will be found even to this day who uses a muzzle loader, such as Kit Carson carried in the middle of the [nineteenth] century. There are exceptions to this rule of the rifle however. In the years after the Civil War one of the many noted hunters of southwest Virginia and east Tennessee was Wilbur Waters, sometimes called The Hunter of White Top. He often killed black bear with a knife and dogs. He spent all his life in hunting and was very successful, killing the last gang of wolves to be found in his neighborhood; and he slew innumerable bears, with no worse results to himself than an occasional bite or scratch.

In the southern states the planters living in the wilder regions have always been in the habit of following the black bear with horse and hound, many of them keeping regular packs of bear hounds. Such a pack includes not only pure-bred hounds, but also cross-bred animals, and some sharp, agile, hard-biting fierce dogs and terriers. They follow the bear and bring him to bay but do not try to kill him, although there are dogs of the big fighting breeds which can readily master a black bear if loosed at him three or four at a time; but the dogs of these southern bear-hound packs are not fitted for such work, and if they try to close with the bear he is certain to play havoc with them, disembowelling them with blows of his paws or seizing them in his arms and biting through their spines or legs. The riders follow the hounds through the canebreaks, and also try to make cutoffs and station themselves at open points where they think the bear will pass, so that they may get a shot at him. The weapons used are rifles, shotguns, and occasionally revolvers.

Sometimes, however, the hunter uses the knife. General Wade Hampton, who has probably killed more black bears than any other man living in the United States, frequently used the knife, slaying thirty or forty with this weapon. His plan was, when he found that the dogs had the bear at bay, to walk up close and cheer them on. They would instantly seize the bear in a body, and he would then rush in and stab it behind the shoulder, reaching over so as to inflict the wound on the opposite side from that where he stood. He escaped scathless from all these encounters save one, in which he was rather severely torn in the forearm. Many other hunters have used the knife, but perhaps none so frequently as he; for he was always fond of steel, as witness his feats with the "white arm" during the Civil War.

General Hampton always hunted with large packs of hounds, managed sometimes by himself and sometimes by his negro hunters. He occasionally took out forty dogs at a time. He found that all his dogs together could not kill a big fat bear, but they occasionally killed three-year-olds, or lean and poor bears. During the course of his life he has himself killed, or been in at the death of, five hundred bears, at least two thirds of them falling by his own hand. In the years just before the war he had on one occasion, in Mississippi, killed sixty-eight bears in five months. Once he killed four bears in a day; at another time three, and frequently two. The two largest bears he himself killed weighed, respectively, 408 and 410 pounds. They were both shot in Mississippi. But he saw at least one bear killed which was much larger than either of these. These figures were taken down at the time, when the animals were actually weighed on the scales. Most of his hunting for bear was done in northern Mississippi, where one of his plantations was situated, near Greenville. During the half century that he hunted, on and off, in this neighborhood, he knew of two instances where hunters were fatally wounded in the chase of the black bear. Both of the men were inexperienced, one being a raftsman who came down the river, and the other a man from Vicksburg. He was not able to learn the particulars in the last case, but the raftsman came too close to a bear that was at bay, and it broke through the dogs, rushed at and overthrew him, then lying on him, it bit him deeply in the thigh, through the femoral artery, so that he speedily bled to death.

But a black bear is not usually a formidable opponent, and though he will sometimes charge home he is much more apt to bluster and bully than actually to come to close quarters. I myself have but once seen a man who had been hurt by one of these bears. This was an Indian. He had come on the beast close up in a thick wood, and had mortally wounded it with his gun; it had then closed with him, knocking the gun out of his hand, so that he was forced to use his knife. It charged him on all fours, but in the grapple, when it had failed to throw him down, it raised itself on its hind legs, clasping him across the shoulders with its fore-paws. Apparently it had no intention of hugging, but merely sought to draw him within reach of his jaws. He fought desperately against this, using the knife freely, and striving to keep its head back; and the flow of blood weakened the animal, so that it finally fell exhausted, before being able dangerously to injure him. But it had bitten his left arm very severely, and its claws had made long gashes on his shoulders.

Black bears, like grizzlies, vary greatly in their modes of attack. Sometimes they rush in and bite; and again they strike with their fore-paws. Two of my cowboys were originally from Maine, where I knew them well. There they were fond of trapping bears, and caught a good many. The huge steel gins, attached by chains to heavy clogs, prevented the trapped beasts from going far; and when found they were always tied tight round some tree or bush, and usually nearly exhausted. The men killed them either with a little 32-calibre pistol or a hatchet. But once did they meet with any difficulty. On this occasion one of them incautiously approached a captured bear to knock it on the head with his hatchet, but the animal managed to partially untwist itself, and with its free fore-arm made a rapid sweep at him; he jumped back just in time, the bear's claws tearing his clothes – after which he shot it. Bears are shy and have very keen noses; they are therefore hard to kill by fair hunting, living, as they generally do, in dense forests or thick brush. They are easy enough to trap, however. Thus, these two men, though they trapped so many, never but once killed them in any other way. On this occasion one of them, in the winter, found in a great hollow log a den where a she and two well-grown cubs had taken up their abode, and shot all three with his rifle as they burst out.

Where they are much hunted, bear become purely nocturnal; but in the wilder forests I have seen them abroad at all hours, though they do not much relish the intense heat of noon. They are rather comical animals to watch feeding and going about the ordinary business of their lives. Once I spent half an hour lying at the edge of a wood and looking at a black bear some three hundred yards off across an open glade. It was in good stalking country, but the wind was unfavorable and I waited for it to shift—waited too long as it proved, for something frightened the beast and he made off before I could get a shot at him. When I first saw him he was shuffling along and rooting in the ground, so that he looked like a great pig. Then he began to turn over the stones and logs to hunt for insects, small reptiles, and the like. A moderate-sized stone he would turn over with a single clap of his paw, and then plunge his nose down into the hollow to gobble up the small creatures beneath while still dazed by the light. The big logs and rocks he would tug and worry at with both paws; once, over-exerting his clumsy strength, he lost his grip and rolled clean on his back. Under some of the logs he evidently found mice and chipmunks; then, as soon as the log was overturned, he would be seen jumping about with grotesque agility, and making quick dabs here and there, as the little, scurrying rodent turned and twisted, until at last he put his paw on it and scooped it up into his mouth. Sometimes, probably when he smelt the mice underneath, he would cautiously turn the log over with one paw, holding the other lifted and ready to strike. Now and then he would halt and sniff the air in every direction and it was after one of these halts that he suddenly shuffled off into the woods.

Black bear generally feed on berries, nuts, insects, carrion, and the like; but at times they take to killing very large animals. In fact, they are curiously irregular in their food. They will kill deer if they can get at them; but generally the deer are too quick. Sheep and hogs are their favorite prey, especially the latter, for bears seem to have a special relish for pork. Twice I have known a black bear kill cattle. Once the victim was a bull which had got mired, and which the bear deliberately proceeded to eat alive, heedless of the bellows of the unfortunate beast. On the other occasion, a cow was surprised and slain among some bushes at the edge of a remote pasture. In the spring, soon after the long winter sleep, they are very hungry, and are especially apt to attack large beasts at this time; although during the very first days of their appearance, when they are just breaking their fast, they eat rather sparingly, and by preference the tender shoots of green grass and other herbs, or frogs and crayfish; it is not for a week or two that they seem to be overcome by lean, ravenous hunger. They will even attack and master that formidable fighter the moose, springing at it from an ambush as it passes—for a bull moose would surely be an overmatch for one of them if fronted fairly in the open. An old hunter, whom I could trust, told me that he had

35

seen in the snow in early spring the place where a bear had sprung at two moose, which were trotting together; he missed his spring, and the moose got off, their strides after they settled down into their pace being tremendous, and showing how thoroughly they were frightened. Another time he saw a bear chase a moose into a lake, where it waded out a little distance, and then turned to bay, bidding defiance to his pursuer, the latter not daring to approach in the water. I have been told—but cannot vouch for it—that instances have been known where the bear, maddened by hunger, has gone in on a moose thus standing at bay, only to be beaten down under the water by the terrible fore-hoofs of the quarry, and to yield its life in the contest. A lumberman told me that he once saw a moose, evidently much startled, trot through a swamp, and immediately afterwards a bear came up following the tracks. He almost ran into the man, and was evidently not in a good temper, for he growled and blustered, and two or three times made feints of charging, before he finally concluded to go off.

Bears will occasionally visit hunters' or lumbermen's camps, in the absence of the owners, and play sad havoc with all that therein is, devouring everything eatable, especially if sweet, and trampling into a dirty mess whatever they do not eat. The black bear does not average more than a third the size of the grizzly; but, like all its kind, it varies greatly in weight. The largest I myself ever saw weighed was in Maine, and tipped the scale at 346 pounds; but I have a perfectly authentic record of one in Maine that weighed 397, and my friend, Dr. Hart Merriam, tells me that he has seen several in the Adirondacks that when killed weighed about 350.

I have myself shot but one or two black bears, and these were obtained under circumstances of no special interest, as I merely stumbled on them while after other game, and killed them before they had a chance either to run or show fight.

"Bear at Elk Carcass," from *Hunting Trips of a Ranchman*.

Old Ephraim, The Grizzly Bear

Chapter II

The king of the game beasts of temperate North America, because the most dangerous to the hunter, is the grizzly bear; known to the few remaining old-time trappers of the Rockies and the Great Plains, sometimes as "Old Ephraim" and sometimes as "Moccasin Joe"—the last in allusion to his queer, half-human footprints, which look as if made by some misshapen giant, walking in moccasins.

Bear vary greatly in size and color, no less than in temper and habits. Old hunters speak much of them in their endless talks over the camp fires and in the snow-bound winter huts. They insist on many species; not merely the black and the grizzly, but the brown, the cinnamon, the gray, the silver-tip, and others with names known only in certain localities, such as the range bear, the roach-back, and the smut-face. But, in spite of popular opinion to the contrary, most old hunters are very untrustworthy in dealing with points of natural history. They usually know only so much about any given game animal as will enable them to kill it. They study its habits solely with this end in view; and once slain they only examine it to see about its condition and fur. With rare exceptions they are quite incapable of passing judgment upon questions of specific identity or difference. When questioned, they not only advance perfectly impossible theories and facts in support of their views, but they rarely even agree as to the views themselves. One hunter will assert that the true grizzly is only found in California, heedless of the fact that the name was first used by Lewis and Clark as one of the titles they applied to the large bears of the plains country round the Upper

Missouri, a quarter of a century before the California grizzly was known to fame. Another hunter will call any big brindled bear a grizzly no matter where it is found; and he and his companions will dispute by the hour as to whether a bear of large, but not extreme, size is a grizzly or a silver-tip. In Oregon the cinnamon bear is a phase of the small black bear; in Montana it is the plains variety of the large mountain silver-tip. I have myself seen the skins of two bears killed on the upper waters of Tongue River; one was that of a male, one of a female, and they had evidently just mated; yet one was distinctly a "silver-tip" and the other a "cinnamon." The skin of one very big bear which I killed in the Bighorn has proved a standing puzzle to almost all the old hunters to whom I have showed it; rarely do any two of them agree as to whether it is a grizzly, a silver-tip, a cinnamon, or a "smut-face." Any bear with unusually long hair on the spine and shoulders, especially if killed in the spring, when the fur is shaggy, is forthwith dubbed a "roach-back." The average sporting writer moreover joins with the more imaginative members of the "old hunter" variety in ascribing wildly various traits to these different bears. One comments on the superior powers of the roach-back; the explanation being that a bear in early spring is apt to be ravenous from hunger. The next insists that the California grizzly is the only really dangerous bear; while another stoutly maintains that it does not compare in ferocity with what he calls the "smaller" silver-tip or cinnamon. And so on, and so on, without end. All of which is mere nonsense.

Nevertheless, it is no easy task to determine how many species or varieties of bear actually do exist in the United States, and I cannot even say without doubt that a very large set of skins and skulls would not show a nearly complete intergradation between the most widely separated individuals. However, there are certainly two very distinct types, which differ almost as widely from each other as a wapiti does from a mule deer, and which exist in the same localities in most heavily timbered portions of the Rockies. One is the small black bear, a bear which will average about two hundred pounds weight, with fine, glossy, black fur, and the fore-claws but little longer than the hinder ones; in fact the hairs of the fore-paw often reach to their tips. This bear is a tree climber. It is the only kind found east of the great plains, and it is also plentiful in the forest-clad portions of the Rockies, being common in most heavily timbered tracts throughout the United States. The other is the grizzly, which weighs three or four times as much as the black, and has a pelt of coarse hair, which is in color gray, grizzled, or brown of various shades. It is not a tree climber, and the fore-claws are very long, much longer than the hinder ones. It is found from the great plains west of the Mississippi to the Pacific coast. This bear inhabits indifferently lowland and mountain; the deep woods, and the barren plains where the only cover is the stunted growth fringing the streams. These two types are very distinct in every way, and their differences are not at all dependent upon mere geographical considerations; for they are often found in the same district. Thus I found them both in the Bighorn Mountains, each type being in extreme form, while the specimens I shot showed no trace of intergradation. The huge grizzled, long-clawed beast, and its little glossy-coated, short-clawed, tree-climbing brother roamed over exactly the same country in those mountains; but they were as distinct in habits, and mixed as little together as moose and caribou.

On the other hand, when a sufficient number of bears, from widely separated regions are examined, the various distinguishing marks are found to be inconstant and to show a tendency—exactly how strong I cannot say—to fade into one another. The differentiation of the two species seems to be as yet scarcely completed; there are more or less imperfect connecting links, and as regards the grizzly it almost seems as if the specific characters were still unstable. In the far northwest, in the basin of the Columbia, the "black" bear is as often brown as any other color; and I have seen the skins of two cubs, one black and one brown, which were shot when following the same dam. When these brown bears have coarser hair than usual their skins are with difficulty to be distinguished from those of certain varieties of the grizzly. Moreover, all bears vary greatly in size; and I have seen the bodies of very large black or brown bears with short fore-claws which were fully as heavy as, or perhaps heavier than, some small but full-grown grizzlies with long fore-claws. These very large bears with short claws are very reluctant to climb a tree; and are almost as clumsy about it as is a young grizzly. Among the grizzlies the fur varies much in color and texture even among bears of the same locality; it is of course richest in the deep forest, while the bears of the dry plains and mountains are of a lighter, more washed-out hue.

A full grown grizzly will usually weigh from five to seven hundred pounds; but exceptional individuals undoubtedly reach more than twelve hundredweight. The California bears are said to be much the largest. This I think is so, but I cannot say it with certainty—at any rate I have examined several skins of full-grown California bears which were no larger than those of many I have seen from the northern Rockies. The Alaskan bears, particularly those of the peninsula, are even bigger beasts; the skin of one which I saw in the possession of Mr. Webster, the taxidermist, was a good deal larger than the average polar bear skin; and the animal when alive, if in good condition, could hardly have weighed less than 1,400 pounds.* Bears vary wonderfully in weight, even to the extent of becoming half as heavy again, according as they are fat or lean; in this respect they are more like hogs than like any other animals.

The grizzly is now chiefly a beast of the high hills and heavy timber; but this is merely because he has learned that he must rely on cover to guard him from man, and has forsaken the open ground accordingly. In old days, and in one or two very out-of-the-way places almost to the present time, he wandered at will over the plains. It is only the wariness born of fear which nowadays causes him to cling to the thick brush of the large river-bottoms throughout the plains country. When there were no rifle-bearing hunters in the land, to harass him and make him afraid, he roved hither and thither at will, in burly self-confidence. Then he cared little for cover, unless as a weather-break, or because it happened to contain food he liked. If the humor seized him he would roam for days over the rolling or broken prairie, searching for roots, digging up gophers, or perhaps following the great buffalo herds either to prey on some unwary straggler which he was able to catch at a disadvantage in a washout, or else to feast on the carcasses of those which died by accident. Old hunters, survivors of the long-vanished ages when the vast herds thronged the high plains and were followed by the wild red tribes, and by bands of whites who were scarcely less savage, have told me that they often met bears under such circumstances; and these bears were accustomed to sleep in a patch of rank sage bush, in the niche of a washout, or under the lee of a boulder, seeking their food abroad even in full daylight. The bears of the Upper Missouri basin—which were so light in color that the early explorers often alluded to them as gray or even as "white"—were particularly given to this life in the open. To this day that close kinsman of the grizzly known as the bear of the barren grounds continues to lead this same kind of life, in the far north. My friend Mr. Rockhill, of Maryland, who was the first white man to explore eastern Tibet, describes the large, grizzly-like bear of those desolate uplands as having similar habits.

However, the grizzly is a shrewd beast and shows the usual bear-like capacity for adapting himself to changed conditions. He has in most places become a cover-haunting animal, sly in his ways, wary to a degree, and clinging to the shelter of the deepest forests in the mountains and of the most tangled thickets in the plains. Hence he has held his own far better than such game as the bison and elk. He is much less common

---

*Both this huge Alaskan bear and the entirely distinct bear of the barren grounds differ widely from the true grizzly, at least in their extreme forms.—T.R.

than formerly, but he is still to be found throughout most of his former range; save of course in the immediate neighborhood of the large towns.

In most places the grizzly hibernates, or as old hunters say "holes up," during the cold season, precisely as does the black bear; but as with the latter species, those animals which live farthest south spend the whole year abroad in mild seasons. The grizzly rarely chooses that favorite den of his little black brother, a hollow tree or log, for his winter sleep, seeking or making some cavernous hole in the ground instead. The hole is sometimes in a slight hillock in a river bottom, but more often on a hillside, and may be either shallow or deep. In the mountains it is generally a natural cave in the rock, but among the foot-hills and on the plains the bear usually has to take some hollow or opening, and then fashion it into a burrow to his liking with his big digging claws.

Before the cold weather sets in the bear begins to grow restless, and to roam about seeking for a good place in which to hole up. One will often try and abandon several caves or partially dug-out burrows in succession before finding a place to its taste. It always endeavors to choose a spot where there is little chance of discovery or molestation, taking great care to avoid leaving too evident trace of its work. Hence it is not often that the dens are found.

Once in its den the bear passes the cold months in lethargic sleep; yet, in all but the coldest weather, and sometimes even then, its slumber is but light, and if disturbed it will promptly leave its den, prepared for fight or flight as the occasion may require. Many times when a hunter has stumbled on the winter resting-place of a bear and has left it, as he thought, without his presence being discovered, he has returned only to find that the crafty old fellow was aware of the danger all the time, and sneaked off as soon as the coast was clear. But in very cold weather hibernating bears can hardly be wakened from their torpid lethargy.

The length of time a bear stays in its den depends of course upon the severity of the season and the latitude and altitude of the country. In the northernmost and coldest regions all the bears hole up, and spend half the year in a state of lethargy; whereas in the south only the she's with young and the fat he-bears retire for the sleep, and these but for a few weeks, and only if the season is severe.

When the bear first leaves its den the fur is in very fine order, but it speedily becomes thin and poor, and does not recover its condition until the fall. Sometimes the bear does not betray any great hunger for a few days after its appearance; but in a short while it becomes ravenous. During the early spring, when the woods are still entirely barren and lifeless, while the snow yet lies in deep drifts, the lean, hungry brute, both maddened and weakened by long fasting, is more of a flesh eater than at any other time. It is at this period that it is most apt to turn true beast of prey, and show its prowess either at the expense of the wild game, or of the flocks of the settler and the herds of the ranchman. Bears are very capricious in this respect, however. Some are confirmed game, and cattle-killers; others are not; while yet others either are or are not accordingly as the freak seizes them, and their ravages vary almost unaccountably, both with the season and the locality.

Throughout 1889, for instance, no cattle, so far as I heard, were killed by bears anywhere near my range on the Little Missouri in western Dakota; yet I happened to know that during that same season the ravages of the bears among the herds of the cowmen in the Big Hole Basin, in western Montana, were very destructive.

In the spring and early summer of 1888, the bears killed no cattle near my ranch; but in the late summer and early fall of that year a big bear, which we well knew by its tracks, suddenly took to cattle-killing. This was a brute which had its headquarters on some very large brush bottoms a dozen miles below my ranch house, and which ranged to and fro across the broken country flanking the river on each side. It began just before berry time, but continued its career of destruction long after the wild plums and even buffalo berries had ripened. I think that what started it was a feast on a cow which had mired and died in the bed of the creek; at least it was not until after we found that it had been feeding at the carcass and had eaten every scrap, that we discovered traces of its ravages among the livestock. It seemed to attack the animals wholly regardless of their size and strength; its victims including a large bull and a beef steer, as well as cows, yearlings, and gaunt, weak trail "doughgies," which had been brought in very late by a Texas cow-outfit—for that year several herds were driven up from the overstocked, eaten-out, and drought-stricken ranges of the far south. Judging from the signs, the crafty old grizzly, as cunning as he was ferocious, usually lay in wait for the cattle when they came down to water, choosing some thicket of dense underbrush and twisted cottonwoods through which they had to pass before reaching the sand banks on the river's brink. Sometimes he pounced on them as they fed through the thick, low cover of the bottoms, where an assailant could either lie in ambush by one of the numerous cattle trails, or else creep unobserved towards some browsing beast. When within a few feet a quick rush carried him fairly on the terrified quarry; and though but a clumsy animal compared to the great cats, the grizzly is far quicker than one would imagine from viewing his ordinary lumbering gait. In one or two instances the bear had apparently grappled with his victim by seizing it near the loins and striking a disabling blow over the small of the back; in at least one instance he had jumped on the animal's head, grasping it with his fore-paws, while with his fangs he tore open the throat or craunched the neck bone. Some of his victims were slain far from the river, in winding, brushy coulies of the Bad Lands, where the broken nature of the ground rendered stalking easy. Several of the ranchmen, angered at their losses, hunted their foe eagerly, but always with ill success; until one of them put poison in a carcass, and thus at last, in ignoble fashion, slew the cattle-killer.

Mr. Clarence King informs me that he was once eyewitness to a bear's killing a steer, in California. The steer was in a small pasture, and the bear climbed over, partly breaking down the rails which barred the gateway. The steer started to run, but the grizzly overtook it in four or five bounds, and struck it a tremendous blow on the flank with one paw, knocking several ribs clear away from the spine, and killing the animal outright by the shock.

Horses no less than horned cattle at times fall victims to this great bear, which usually spring on them from the edge of a clearing as they graze in some mountain pasture, or among the foot-hills; and there is no other animal of which horses seem so much afraid. Generally the bear, whether successful or unsuccessful in its raids on cattle and horses, comes off unscathed from the struggle; but this is not always the case, and it has much respect for the hoofs or horns of its should-be prey. Some horses do not seem to know how to fight at all; but others are both quick and vicious, and prove themselves very formidable foes, lashing out behind, and striking with their fore-hoofs. I have elsewhere given an instance of a stallion which beat off a bear, breaking its jaw.

Quite near my ranch, once, a cowboy in my employ found unmistakable evidence of the discomfiture of a bear by a long-horned range cow. It was in the early spring, and the cow with her new-born calf was in a brush-bordered valley. The footprints in the damp soil were very plain, and showed all that had happened. The bear had evidently come out of the bushes with a rush, probably bent merely on seizing the calf; and had slowed up when the cow instead of flying faced him. He had then begun to walk round his expected dinner in a circle, the cow fronting him and moving nervously back and forth, so that her sharp hoofs cut and trampled the ground. Finally she had charged savagely; whereupon the bear had bolted; and whether frightened at the charge, or at the approach of some one, he had not returned.

The grizzly is even fonder of sheep and pigs than is its smaller black brother. Lurking round the settler's house until after nightfall, it will vault into the fold or sty, grasp a helpless, bleating fleece-bearer, or a shrieking, struggling member of the bristly brotherhood, and bundle it out over the fence to its death. In carrying its prey a bear sometimes holds the body in its teeth, walking along on all-fours and dragging it as a wolf does. Sometimes, however, it seizes an animal in its forearms or in one of them, and walks awkwardly on three legs or two, adopting this method in lifting and pushing the body over rocks and down timber.

When a grizzly can get at domestic animals it rarely seeks to molest game, the former being far less wary and more helpless. Its heaviness and clumsiness do not fit it well for a life of rapine against shy woodland creatures. Its vast strength and determined temper, however, more than make amends for lack of agility in the actual struggle with the stricken prey; its difficulty lies in seizing, not in killing, the game. Hence, when a grizzly does take to game-killing, it is likely to attack bison, moose, and elk; it is rarely able to catch deer, still less sheep or antelope. In fact these smaller game animals often show but little dread of its neighborhood, and, though careful not to let it come too near, go on grazing when a bear is in full sight. Whitetail deer are frequently found at home in the same thicket in which a bear has its den, while they immediately desert the temporary abiding place of a wolf or cougar. Nevertheless, they sometimes presume too much on this confidence. A couple of years before the occurrence of the feats of cattle-killing mentioned above as happening near my ranch, either the same bear that figured in them, or another of similar tastes, took to game-hunting. The beast lived in the same succession of huge thickets which cover for two or three miles the river bottoms and the mouths of the inflowing creeks; and he suddenly made a raid on the whitetail deer which were plentiful in the dense cover. The shaggy, clumsy monster was cunning enough to kill several of these knowing creatures. The exact course of procedure I never could find out; but apparently the bear laid in wait beside the game trails, along which the deer wandered.

In the old days when the innumerable bison grazed free on the prairie, the grizzly sometimes harassed their bands as it now does the herds of the ranchman. The bison was the most easily approached of all game, and the great bear could often get near some outlying straggler, in its quest after stray cows, yearlings, or calves. In default of a favorable chance to make a prey of one of these weaker members of the herds, it did not hesitate to attack the mighty bulls themselves; and perhaps the grandest sight which it was ever the good fortune of the early hunters to witness, was one of these rare battles between a hungry grizzly and a powerful buffalo bull. Nowadays, however, the few last survivors of the bison are vanishing even from the inaccessible mountain fastnesses in which they sought a final refuge from their destroyers.

At present the wapiti is of all wild game that which is most likely to fall a victim to the grizzly, when the big bear is in the mood to turn hunter. Wapiti are found in the same places as the grizzly, and in some spots they are yet very plentiful; they are less shy and active than deer, while not powerful enough to beat off so ponderous a foe; and they live in cover where there is always a good chance either to stalk or to stumble on them. At almost any season bear will come and feast on an elk carcass; and if the food supply runs short, in early spring, or in a fall when the berry crop fails, they sometimes have to do their own killing. Twice I have come across the remains of elk, which had seemingly been slain and devoured by bears. I have never heard of elk making a fight against a bear; yet, at close quarters and at bay, a bull elk in the rutting season is an ugly foe.

A bull moose is even more formidable, being able to strike the most lightning-like blows with his terrible forefeet, his true weapons of defense. I doubt if any beast of prey would rush in on one of these wood-land giants, when his horns were grown, and if he was on his guard and bent on fight. Nevertheless, the moose sometimes fall victims to the uncouth prowess of the grizzly, in the thick wet forests of the high northern Rockies, where both beasts dwell. An old hunter who a dozen years ago wintered at Jackson Lake, in northwestern Wyoming, told me that when the snows got deep on the mountains the moose came down and took up their abode near the lake, on its western side. Nothing molested them during the winter. Early in the spring a grizzly came out of its den, and he found its tracks in many places, as it roamed restlessly about, evi-dently very hungry. Finding little to eat in the bleak, snow-drifted woods, it soom began to depredate on the moose, and killed two or three, generally by lying in wait and dashing out on them as they passed near its lurking-place. Even the bulls were at that season weak, and of course hornless, with small desire to fight; and in each case the rush of the great bear—doubtless made with the ferocity and speed which so often belie the seeming awkwardness of the animal—bore down the startled victim, taken utterly unawares before it had a chance to defend itself. In one case the bear had missed its spring; the moose going off, for a few rods, with huge jumps, and then settling down into its characteristic trot. The old hunter who followed the tracks said he would never have deemed it possible for any animal to make such strides while in a trot.

Nevertheless, the grizzly is only occasionally, not normally, a formidable predatory beast, a killer of cattle and of large game. Although

capable of far swifter movement than is promised by his frame of seemingly clumsy strength, and in spite of his power of charging with astonishing suddenness and speed, he yet lacks altogether the supple agility of
such finished destroyers as the cougar and the wolf; and for the absence
of this agility no amount of mere huge muscle can atone. He is more apt
to feast on animals which have met their death by accident, or which
have been killed by other beasts or by man, than to do his own killing.
He is a very foul feeder, with a strong relish for carrion, and possesses
a gruesome and cannibal fondness for the flesh of his own kind; a bear
carcass will toll a brother bear to the ambushed hunter better than almost
any other bait, unless it is the carcass of a horse.

Nor do these big bears always content themselves merely with
the carcasses of their brethren. A black bear would have a poor chance
if in the clutches of a large, hungry grizzly; and an old male will kill and
eat a cub, especially if he finds it at a disadvantage. A rather remarkable
instance of this occurred in the Yellowstone National Park, in the spring
of 1891. The incident is related in the following letter written to Mr.
William Hallett Phillips, of Washington, by another friend, Mr. Elwood
Hofer. Hofer is an old mountain-man; I have hunted with him myself,
and know his statements to be trustworthy. He was, at the time, at work
in the Park getting animals for the National Museum at Washington, and
was staying at Yancey's "hotel" near Tower Fall. His letter which was
dated June 21st, 1891, runs in part as follows:

"I had a splendid Grizzly or Roachback cub and was going to send
him into the Springs next morning the team was here, I heard a racket
out side went out and found him dead an old bear that made an 9½ inch
track had killed and partly eaten him. Last night another one came, one
that made an 8½ inch track, and broke Yancy up in the milk business.
You know how the cabins stand here. There is a hitching post between
the saloon and old house, the little bear was killed there. In a creek close
by was a milk house, last night another bear came there and smashed
the whole thing up, leaving nothing but a few flattened buckets and pans
and boards. I was sleeping in the old cabin, I heard the tin ware rattle
but thought it was all right [and] supposed it was cows or horses about.
I don't care about the milk but the damn cuss dug up the remains of
the cub I had buried in the old ditch, he visited the old meat house but
found nothing. Bear are very thick in this part of the Park, and are getting very fresh. I sent in the game to Capt. Anderson, hear it's doing well."

Grizzlies are fond of fish; and on the Pacific slope, where the salmon
run, they, like so many other beasts, travel many scores of miles and
crowd down to the rivers to gorge themselves upon the fish which are

thrown up on the banks. Wading into the water a bear will knock out the salmon right and left when they are running thick.

Flesh and fish do not constitute the grizzly's ordinary diet. At most times the big bear is a grubber in the ground, an eater of insects, roots, nuts, and berries. Its dangerous fore-claws are normally used to overturn stones and knock rotten logs to pieces, that it may lap up the small tribes of darkness which swarm under the one and in the other. It digs up the camas roots, wild onions, and an occasional luckless woodchuck or gopher. If food is very plenty bears are lazy, but commonly they are obliged to be very industrious, it being no light task to gather enough ants, beetles, crickets, tumble-bugs, roots, and nuts to satisfy the cravings of so huge a bulk. The sign of a bear's work is, of course, evident to the most unpracticed eye; and in no way can one get a better idea of the brute's power than by watching it busily working for its breakfast, shattering big logs and upsetting boulders by sheer strength. There is always a touch of the comic, as well as a touch of the strong and terrible, in a bear's look and actions. It will tug and pull, now with one paw, now with two, now on all fours, now on its hind legs, in the effort to turn over a large log or stone; and when it succeeds it jumps round to thrust its muzzle into the damp hollow and lap up the affrighted mice or beetles while they are still paralyzed by the sudden exposure.

The true time of plenty for bears is the berry season. Then they feast ravenously on huckleberries, blueberries, kinnikinic berries, buffalo berries, wild plums, elderberries, and scores of other fruits. They often smash all the bushes in a berry patch, gathering the fruit with half-luxurious, half-laborious greed, sitting on their haunches, and sweeping the berries into their mouths with dexterous paws. So absorbed do they become in their feasts on the luscious fruit that they grow reckless of their safety, and feed in broad daylight, almost at midday; while in some of the thickets, especially those of the mountain haws, they make so much noise in smashing the branches that it is a comparatively easy matter to approach them unheard. That still-hunter is in luck who in the fall finds an accessible berry-covered hill-side which is haunted by bears; but, as a rule, the berry bushes do not grow close enough together to give the hunter much chance.

Like most other wild animals, bears which have known the neighborhood of man are beasts of the darkness, or at least of the dusk and the gloaming. But they are by no means such true night-lovers as the big cats and the wolves. In regions where they know little of hunters they roam about freely in the daylight, and in cool weather are even apt to take their noontide slumbers basking in the sun. Where they are much hunted they finally almost reverse their natural habits and sleep throughout the hours of light, only venturing abroad after nightfall and before sunrise; but even yet this is not the habit of those bears which exist in the wilder localities where they are still plentiful. In these places they sleep, or at least rest, during the hours of greatest heat, and again in the middle part of the night, unless there is a full moon. They start on their rambles for food about mid-afternoon, and end their morning roaming soon after the sun is above the horizon. If the moon is full, however, they may feed all night long, and then wander but little in the daytime.

Aside from man, the full-grown grizzly has hardly any foe to fear. Nevertheless, in the early spring, when weakened by the hunger that succeeds the winter sleep, it behooves even the grizzly, if he dwells in the mountain fastnesses of the far northwest, to beware of a famished troop of great timber wolves. These northern Rocky Mountain wolves are most formidable beasts, and when many of them band together in time of famine they do not hesitate to pounce on the black bear and cougar; and even a full-grown grizzly is not safe from their attacks, unless he can back up against some rock which will prevent them from assailing him from behind. A small ranchman whom I knew well, who lived near Flathead Lake, once in April found where a troop of these wolves had killed a good-sized yearling grizzly. Either cougar or wolf will make a prey of a grizzly which is but a few months old; while any fox, lynx, wolverine, or fisher will seize the very young cubs. The old story about wolves fearing to feast on game killed by a grizzly is all nonsense. Wolves are canny beasts, and they will not approach a carcass if they think a bear is hidden nearby and likely to rush out at them; but under ordinary circumstances they will feast not only on the carcasses of the grizzly's victims, but on the carcass of the grizzly himself after he has been slain and left by the hunter. Of course wolves would only attack a grizzly if in the most desperate straits for food, as even a victory over such an antagonist must be purchased with heavy loss of life; and a hungry grizzly would devour either a wolf or a cougar, or any one of the smaller carnivora off-hand if it happened to corner it where it could not get away.

The grizzly occasionally makes its den in a cave and spends therein the midday hours. But this is rare. Usually it lies in the dense shelter of the most tangled piece of woods in the neighborhood, choosing by preference some bit where the young growth is thick and the ground strewn with boulders and fallen logs. Often, especially if in a restless mood and roaming much over the country, it merely makes a temporary bed, in which it lies but once or twice; and again it may make a more permanent lair or series of lairs, spending many consecutive nights in each. Usually the lair or bed is made some distance from the feeding ground; but bold bears, in very wild localities, may lie close by a carcass, or in the middle of a berry ground. The deer-killing bear above mentioned had evidently dragged two or three of his victims to his den, which was under an impenetrable mat of bull-berries and dwarf box-alders, hemmed in by a cut bank on one side and a wall of gnarled cottonwoods on the other. Round this den, and rendering it noisome, were scattered the bones of several deer and a young steer or heifer. When we found it we thought we could easily kill the bear, but the fierce, cunning beast must have seen or smelt us, for though we laid in wait for it long and patiently, it did not come back to its place; nor, on our subsequent visits, did we ever find traces of its having done so.

Bear are fond of wallowing in the water, whether in the sand, on the edge of a rapid plains river, on the muddy margin of a pond, or in the oozy moss of a clear, cold mountain spring. One hot August afternoon, as I was clambering down a steep mountain-side near Pend-Oreille Lake, I heard a crash some distance below, which showed that a large beast was afoot. On making my way towards the spot, I found I had disturbed a big bear as it was lolling at ease in its bath; the discolored water showed where it had scrambled hastily out and galloped off as I approached. The spring welled out at the base of a high granite rock, forming a small pool of shimmering broken crystal. The soaked moss lay in a deep wet cushion round about, and jutted over the edges of the pool like a floating shelf. Graceful, water-loving ferns swayed to and fro. Above, the great conifers spread their murmuring branches, dimming the light, and keeping out the heat; their brown boles sprang from the ground like buttressed columns. On the barren mountainside beyond the heat was oppressive. It was small wonder that Bruin should have sought the spot to cool his gross carcass in the fresh spring water.

The bear is a solitary beast, and although many may assemble together, in what looks like a drove, on some favorite feeding-ground—usually where the berries are thick, or by the banks of a salmon-thronged river—the association is never more than momentary, each going its own way as soon as its hunger is satisfied. The males always live alone by choice, save in the rutting season, when they seek the females. Then two or three may come together in the course of their pursuit and rough courtship of the female; and if the rivals are well matched, savage battles follow, so that many of the old males have their heads seamed with scars made by their fellows' teeth. At such times they are evil tempered and prone to attack man or beast on slight provocation.

The she brings forth her cubs, one, two, or three in number, in her winter den. They are very small and helpless things, and it is some time after she leaves her winter home before they can follow her for any distance. They stay with her throughout the summer and the fall, leaving her when the cold weather sets in. By this time they are well grown; and hence, especially if an old male has joined the she, the family may number three or four individuals, so as to make what seems like quite a little troop of bears. A small ranchman who lived a dozen miles from me on the Little Missouri once found a she-bear and three half-grown cubs feeding at a berry-patch in a ravine. He shot the old she in the small of the back, whereat she made a loud roaring and squealing. One of the cubs rushed towards her; but its sympathy proved misplaced, for she knocked it over with a hearty cuff, either out of mere temper, or because she thought her pain must be due to an unprovoked assault from one of her offspring. The hunter then killed one of the cubs, and the other two escaped. When bears are together and one is wounded by a bullet, but does not see the real assailant, it often falls tooth and nail upon its comrade, apparently attributing its injury to the latter.

Bears are hunted in many ways. Some are killed by poison; but this plan is only practical by the owners of cattle or sheep who have suffered from their ravages. Moreover, they are harder to poison than wolves. Most often they are killed in traps, which are sometimes deadfalls, on the principle of the little figure-4 trap familiar to every American country boy, sometimes log-pens in which the animal is taken alive, but generally huge steel gins. In some states there is a bounty for the destruction of grizzlies; and in many places their skins have a market price, although much less valuable than those of the black bear. The men who pursue them for the bounty, or for their fur, as well as the ranchmen who regard them as foes to stock, ordinarily use steel traps. The trap is very massive, needing no small strength to set, and it is usually chained to a bar or log of wood, which does not stop the bear's progress outright, but hampers and interferes with it, continually catching in tree stumps and the like. The animal when trapped makes off at once, biting at the trap and the bar; but it leaves a broad wake and sooner or later is found tangled up by the chain and bar. A bear is by no means so difficult to trap as a wolf or fox although more so than a cougar or a lynx. In wild regions a skillful trapper can often catch a great many with comparative ease. A cunning old grizzly however, soon learns the danger, and is then almost impossible to trap, as it either avoids the neighborhood altogether or finds out some way by which to get at the bait without springing the trap, or else deliberately springs it first. I have been told of bears which spring traps by rolling across them, the iron jaws slipping harmlessly off the big round body. An old horse is the most common bait.

It is, of course, all right to trap bears when they are followed merely as vermin or for the sake of the fur. Occasionally, however, hunters who are out merely for sport adopt this method; but this should never be done. To shoot a trapped bear for sport is a thoroughly unsportsmanlike proceeding. A funny plea sometimes advanced in its favor is that it is "dangerous." No doubt in exceptional instances this is true; exactly as it is true that in exceptional instances it is "dangerous" for a butcher to knock over a steer in the slaughter-house. A bear caught only by the toes may wrench itself free as the hunter comes near, and attack him with pain-maddened fury; or if followed at once, and if the trap and bar are light, it may be found in some thicket, still free, and in a frenzy of rage. But even in such cases the beast has been crippled, and though crazy with pain and anger is easily dealt with by a good shot; while ordinarily the poor brute is found in the last stages of exhaustion, tied tight to a tree where the log or bar has caught, its teeth broken to splintered stumps by rabid snaps at the cruel trap and chain. Some trappers kill the trapped grizzlies with a revolver; so that it may easily be seen that the sport is not normally dangerous. Two of my own cowboys, Sewell and Dow, were originally from Maine, where they had trapped a number of black bears; and they always killed them either with a hatchet or a small 32-calibre revolver. One of them, Sewell, once came near being mauled by a trapped bear, seemingly at the last gasp, which he approached incautiously with his hatchet.

There is, however, one very real danger to which the solitary bear-trapper is exposed, the danger of being caught in his own trap. The huge jaws of the gin are easy to spring and most hard to open. If an unwary passer-by should tread between them and be caught by the leg, his fate would be doubtful, though he would probably die under the steadily growing torment of the merciless iron jaws, as they pressed ever deeper into the sore flesh and broken bones. But if caught by the arms, while setting or fixing the trap, his fate would be in no doubt at all, for it would be impossible for the stoutest man to free himself by any means. Terrible stories are told of solitary mountain hunters who disappeared, and were found years later in the lonely wilderness, as mouldering skeletons, the shattered bones of the forearms still held in the rusty jaws of the gin.

Doubtless the grizzly could be successfully hunted with dogs, if the latter were carefully bred and trained to the purpose, but as yet this has not been done, and though dogs are sometimes used as adjuncts in grizzly hunting they are rarely of much service. It is sometimes said that very small dogs are the best for this end. But this is only so with grizzlies that have never been hunted. In such a case the big bear sometimes becomes so irritated with the bouncing, yapping little terriers or fice-dogs that he may try to catch them and thus permit the hunter to creep upon him. But the minute he realizes, as he speedily does, that the man is his real foe, he pays no further heed whatever to the little dogs, who can then neither bring him to bay nor hinder his flight. Ordinary hounds, of the kinds used in the South for fox, deer, wildcat, and black bear, are but little better. I have known one or two men who at different times tried to hunt the grizzly with a pack of hounds and fice-dogs wonted to the chase of the black bear, but they never met with success. This was probably largely owing to the nature of the country in which they hunted, a vast tangled mass of forest and craggy mountain; but it was also due to the utter inability of the dogs to stop the quarry from breaking bay when it wished. Several times a grizzly was bayed, but always in some inaccessible spot which it took hard climbing to reach, and the dogs were never able to hold the beast until the hunters came up.

Still a well-trained pack of large hounds which were both bold and cunning could doubtless bay even a grizzly. Such dogs are the big half-breed hounds sometimes used in the Alleghanies of West Virginia, which are trained not merely to nip a bear, but to grip him by the hock as he runs and either throw him or twirl him round. A grizzly could not disregard a wary and powerful hound capable of performing this trick, even though he paid small heed to mere barking and occasional nipping. Nor do I doubt that it would be possible to get together a pack of many large, fierce dogs, trained to dash straight at the head and hold on like a vice, which would fairly master a grizzly and, though unable, of course, to kill him, would worry him breathless and hold him down so that he could be slain with ease. There have been instances in which five or six of the big so-called blood-hounds of the southern states—not pure blood-hounds at all, but huge, fierce, ban-dogs, with a cross of the ferocious Cuban blood-hound, to give them good scenting powers—have by themselves mastered the cougar and the black bear. Such instances occurred in the hunting history of my own forefathers on my mother's side, who during the last half of the eighteenth, and the first half of the present [nineteenth], century lived in Georgia and over the border in what are now Alabama and Florida. These big dogs can only overcome such foes by rushing in in a body and grappling all together; if they hang back, lunging and snapping, a cougar or bear will destroy them one by one. With a quarry so huge and redoubtable as the grizzly, no number of dogs, however large and fierce, could overcome him unless they all rushed on him in a mass, the first in the charge seizing by the head or throat. If the dogs hung back, or if there were only a few of them, or if they did not seize around the head, they would be destroyed without an effort. It is murder to slip merely one or two close-quarter dogs at a grizzly. Twice I have known a man take a large bull dog with his pack when after one of these big bears, and in each case the result was the same. In one instance the bear was trotting when the bulldog seized it by the cheek, and without so much as altering its gait, it brushed off the hanging dog with a blow from the fore-paw that broke the latter's back. In the other instance the bear had come to bay, and when seized by the ear it got the dog's body up to its jaws, and tore out the life with one crunch.

A small number of dogs must rely on their activity, and must hamper the bear's escape by inflicting a severe bite and avoiding the counter-stroke. The only dog I ever heard of which, single-handed, was really of service in stopping a grizzly, was a big Mexican sheep-dog, once owned by the hunter Tazewell Woody. It was an agile beast with powerful jaws, and possessed both intelligence and a fierce, resolute temper. Woody killed three grizzlies with its aid. It attacked with equal caution and ferocity, rushing at the bear as the latter ran, and seizing the outstretched hock with a grip of iron, stopping the bear short, but letting go before the angry beast could whirl round and seize it. It was so active and wary that it always escaped damage; and it was so strong and bit so severely that the bear could not possibly run from it at any speed. In consequence, if it once came to close quarters with its quarry, Woody could always get near enough for a shot.

Hitherto, however, the mountain hunters—as distinguished from the trappers—who have followed the grizzly have relied almost solely on their rifles. In my own case about half the bears I have killed I stumbled across almost by accident; and probably this proportion holds good generally. The hunter may be after bear at the time, or he may be after blacktail deer or elk, the common game in most of the haunts of the grizzly; or he may merely be travelling through the country or prospecting for gold. Suddenly he comes over the edge of a cut bank, or round the sharp spur of a mountain or the shoulder of a cliff which walls in a ravine, or else the indistinct game trail he has been following through the great trees twists sharply to one side to avoid a rock or a mass of down timber, and behold he surprises old Ephraim digging for roots, or munching berries, or slouching along the path, or perhaps rising suddenly from the lush, rank plants amid which he has been lying. Or it may be that the bear will be spied afar rooting in an open glade or on a bare hillside.

In the still-hunt proper it is necessary to find some favorite feeding-ground, where there are many roots or berry-bearing bushes, or else to lure the grizzly to a carcass. This last method of "baiting" for bear is under ordinary circumstances the only way which affords even a moderately fair chance of killing them. They are very cunning, with the sharpest of noses, and where they have had experience of hunters they dwell only in cover where it is almost impossible for the best of still-hunters to approach them.

Nevertheless, in favorable ground a man can often find and kill them by fair stalking, in berry time, or more especially in the early spring, before the snow has gone from the mountains, and while the bears are driven by hunger to roam much abroad and sometimes to seek their food in the open. In such cases the still-hunter is stirring by the earliest dawn, and walks with stealthy speed to some high point of observation from which he can overlook the feeding-grounds where he has previously discovered sign. From the coign of vantage he scans the country far and near, either with his own keen eyes or with powerful glasses; and he must combine patience and good sight with the ability to traverse long distances noiselessly and yet at speed. He may spend two or three hours sitting still and looking over a vast tract of country before he will suddenly spy a bear; or he may see nothing after the most careful search in a given place, and must then go on half a dozen miles to another, watching warily as he walks, and continuing this possibly for several days before getting a glimpse of his game. If the bear are digging roots, or otherwise procuring their food on the bare hillsides and table-lands, it is of course comparatively easy to see them; and it is under such circumstances that this kind of hunting is most successful. Once seen, the actual stalk may take two or three hours, the nature of the ground and the direction of the wind often necessitating a long circuit; perhaps a gully, a rock, or a fallen log offers a chance for an approach to within two hundred yards, and although the hunter will, if possible, get much closer than this, yet even at such a distance a bear is a large enough mark to warrant risking a shot.

Usually the berry grounds do not offer such favorable opportunities, as they often lie in thick timber, or are covered so densely with bushes as to obstruct the view; and they are rarely commanded by a favorable spot from which to spy. On the other hand, as already said, bears occasionally forget all their watchfulness while devouring fruit, and make such a noise rending and tearing the bushes that, if once found, a man can creep upon them unobserved.

"A Cowboy and Bear Fight," from *The Wilderness Hunter.*

The Bear's Disposition
Chapter III

My own experience with bears tends to make me lay special emphasis upon their variation in temper. There are savage and cowardly bears, just as there are big and little ones; and sometimes these variations are very marked among bears of the same district, and at other times all the bears of one district will seem to have a common code of behavior which differs utterly from that of the bears of another district. Readers of Lewis and Clark do not need to be reminded of the great difference they found in ferocity between the bears of the Upper Missouri and the bears of the Columbia River drainage system; and those who have lived in the Upper Missouri country nowadays know how widely the bears that still remain have altered in character from what they were as recently as the middle of the century.

This variability has been shown in the bears which I have stumbled upon at close quarters. On but one occasion was I ever regularly charged by a grizzly. To this animal I had given a mortal wound, and without any effort at retaliation he bolted into a thicket of what, in my hurry, I thought was laurel (it being composed in reality I suppose of thick-growing berry bushes). On my following him up and giving him a second wound, he charged very determinedly, taking two bullets without flinching. I just escaped the charge by jumping to one side, and he died almost immediately after striking at me as he rushed by. This bear charged with his mouth open, but made very little noise after the growl or roar with which he greeted my second bullet. I mention the fact of his having kept his mouth open, because one or two of my friends who have been charged have informed me that in their cases they particularly noticed that the bear charged with his mouth shut. Perhaps the fact that my bear was shot through the lungs may account for the difference, or it may simply be another example of individual variation.

On another occasion, in a windfall, I got up within eight or ten feet of a grizzly, which simply bolted off, paying no heed to a hurried shot which I delivered as I poised unsteadily on the swaying top of an overthrown dead pine. On yet another occasion, when I roused a big bear from his sleep, he at the first moment seemed to pay little or no heed to me, and then turned toward me in a leisurely way, the only sign of hostility he betrayed being to ruffle up the hair on his shoulders and the back of his neck. I hit him square between the eyes, and he dropped like a pole-axed steer.

On another occasion I got up quite close to and mortally wounded a bear, which ran off without uttering a sound until it fell dead; but another of these grizzlies, which I shot from ambush, kept squalling and yelling every time I hit him, making a great rumpus. On one occasion one of my cow hands and myself were able to run down on foot a she grizzly bear and her cub, which had obtained a long start of us, simply because of the foolish conduct of the mother. The cub—or more properly the yearling, for it was a cub of the second year—ran on far ahead, and would have escaped if the old she had not continually stopped and sat up on her hind legs to look back at us. I think she did this partly from curiosity, but partly also from bad temper, for once or twice she grinned and roared at us. The upshot of it was that I got within range and put a bullet in the old she, who afterwards charged my companion and was killed, and we also got the yearling.

Another young grizzly which I killed dropped to the first bullet, which entered its stomach. It then let myself and my companion approach closely, looking up at us with alert curiosity, but making no effort to escape. It was really not crippled at all, but we thought from its actions that its back was broken, and my companion foolishly advanced to kill it with his pistol. The pistol, however, did not inflict a mortal wound, and the only effect was to make the young bear jump to its feet as if unhurt, and race off at full speed through the timber; for though not full-grown it was beyond cubhood, being probably about eighteen months old. By desperate running I succeeded in getting another shot, and more by luck than anything else knocked it over, this time permanently.

Black bear are not, under normal conditions, formidable brutes.

They are not nearly so apt to charge as is a wild hog; but if they do charge and get home they will maul a man severely, and there are a number of instances on record in which they have killed men. Ordinarily, however, a black bear will not charge at all, though he may bluster a good deal. I once shot one very close up which made a most lamentable outcry, and seemed to lose its head, its efforts to escape resulting in its bouncing about among the trees with such heedless hurry that I was easily able to kill it. Another black bear, which I also shot at close quarters, came straight for my companions and myself, and almost ran over the white hunter who was with me. This bear made no sound whatever when I first hit it, and I do not think it was charging. I believe it was simply dazed, and by accident ran the wrong way, and so almost came into collision with us. However, when it found itself face to face with the white hunter, and only four or five feet away, it prepared for hostilities, and I think would have mauled him if I had not brained it with another bullet; for I was myself standing but six feet or so to one side of it.

Ordinarily, however, my experience has been that bears were not flurried when I suddenly came upon them. They impressed me as if they were always keeping in mind the place toward which they wished to retreat in the event of danger, and for this place, which was invariably a piece of rough ground or dense timber, they made off with all possible speed, not seeming to lose their heads.

Frequently I have been able to watch bears for some time while myself unobserved. With other game I have very often done this even when within close range, not wishing to kill creatures needlessly, or without a good object; but with bears, my experience has been that chances to secure them come so seldom as to make it very distinctly worth while improving any that do come, and I have not spent much time watching any bear unless he was in a place where I could not get at him, or else was so close at hand that I was not afraid of his getting away. On one occasion the bear was hard at work digging up squirrel or gopher caches on the side of a pine-clad hill. He looked rather like a big badger when so engaged. On two other occasions the bear was working around a carcass preparatory to burying it. On these occasions I was very close, and it was extremely interesting to note the grotesque, half human movements, and giant, awkward strength of the great beast. He would twist the carcass around with the utmost ease, sometimes taking it in his teeth and dragging it, at other times grasping it in his forepaws and half lifting, half shoving it. Once the bear lost his grip and rolled over during the course of some movement, and this made him angry, and he struck the carcass a savage whack, just as a pettish child will strike a table against which it has knocked itself.

At another time I watched a black bear some distance off getting his breakfast under stumps and stones. He was very active, turning the stone or log over, and then thrusting his muzzle into the empty space to gobble up the small creatures below before they recovered from the surprise and the sudden inflow of light. From under one log he put up a chipmunk, and danced hither and thither with even more agility than awkwardness, slapping at the chipmunk with his paw while it zigzagged about, until finally he scooped it into his mouth.

The Yellowstone Park now presents the best chance for observing the habits of bears that has ever been offered, for though they are wild in theory, yet in practice they have come to frequenting the hotels at dusk and after nightfall, as if they were half tame at least; and it is earnestly to be wished that some Boone and Crockett member who, unlike the present writer, does not belong to the laboring classes, would devote a month or two, or indeed a whole season, to the serious study of the life history of these bears. It would be time very well spent.

"Grizzly Killing a Steer," from *The Wilderness Hunter*.

A Cattle-Killing Bear

Chapter IV

There were, in 1897, a few grizzlies left here and there along the Little Missouri, usually in large bottoms covered with an almost impenetrable jungle of timber and thorny brush. In the old days they used to be very plentiful in this region, and ventured boldly out on the prairie. The Little Missouri region was a famous hunting-ground for both the white trappers and the Indian hunters in those old days when the far West was still a wilderness, and the men who trapped beaver would wander for years over the plains and mountains and see no white faces save those of their companions.

Indeed, at that time the Little Missouri was very dangerous country, as it was the debatable-ground between many powerful Indian tribes, and was only visited by formidable war-parties and hunting-parties. In consequence of nobody daring to live there, game swarmed—buffalo, elk, deer, antelope, mountain-sheep, and bear. The bears were then very bold, and the hunters had little difficulty in getting up to them, for they were quite as apt to attack as to run away.

But when, in 1880, the Northern Pacific Railroad reached the neighborhood of the Little Missouri, all this changed forever. The game that for untold ages had trodden out their paths over the prairies and along the river-bottoms vanished, as the Indians that had hunted it also vanished. The bold white hunters also passed away with the bears they had chased and the red foes against whom they had warred. In their places the ranchman came in with great herds of cattle and horses and flocks of sheep, and built their log cabins and tilled their scanty garden-patches, and cut down the wild hay for winter fodder. Now bears are as shy as they are scarce. No grizzly in such a settled region would dream of attacking a man unprovoked, and they pass their days in the deepest thickets, so that it is almost impossible to get at them. I never killed a bear in the neighborhood of my former ranch, though I have shot quite a number some hundreds of miles to the west in the Rocky Mountains.

Usually the bears live almost exclusively on roots, berries, insects, and the like. In fact, there is always something grotesque and incongruous in comparing the bear's vast size, and his formidable claws and teeth, with the uses to which those claws and teeth are normally put. At the end of the season the claws, which are very long in spring, sometimes become so much blunted as to be tender, because the bear has worked on hard ground digging roots and the like.

Bears often graze on the fresh tender spring grass. Berries form their especial delight, and they eat them so greedily when in season as to become inordinately fat. Indeed, a bear in a berry-patch frequently grows so absorbed in his work as to lose his wariness, and as he makes a good deal of noise himself in breaking branches and gobbling down the fruit, he is exposed to much danger from the hunter.

Besides roots and berries, the bear will feed on any small living thing he encounters. If in plundering a squirrel's cache he comes upon some young squirrels, down they go in company with the hoarded nuts. He is continually knocking to pieces and overturning old dead logs for the sake of devouring the insects living beneath them. If, when such a log is overturned, mice, shrews, or chipmunks are found underneath, the bear promptly scoops them into his mouth while they are still dazed by the sudden inrush of light. All this seems rather ludicrous as the life work of an animal of such huge proportions and such vast strength.

Sometimes, however, a bear will take to killing fresh meat for itself. Indeed, I think it is only its clumsiness that prevents it from becoming an habitual flesh-eater. Deer are so agile that bears can rarely get them; yet on occasions not only deer, but moose, buffalo, and elk fall victims to them. Wild game, however, are so shy, so agile, and so alert that it is only rarely they afford meals to old Ephraim—as the mountain hunters call the grizzly.

Domestic animals are slower, more timid, more clumsy, and with far duller senses. It is on these that the bear by preference preys when he needs fresh meat. I have never, myself, known one to kill horses;

but I have been informed that the feat is sometimes performed, usually in spring; and the ranchman who told me insisted that when a bear made his rush he went with such astonishing speed that the horse was usually overtaken before it got well under way.

The favorite food of a bear, however, if he really wants fresh meat, is a hog or sheep—by preference the former. If a bear once gets into the habit of visiting a sheepfold or pigpen, it requires no slight skill and watchfulness to keep him out. As for swine, they dread bears more than anything else. A drove of half-wild swine will make head against a wolf or panther; but the bear scatters them in a panic. This feat is entirely justifiable, for a bear has a peculiar knack in knocking down a hog, and then literally eating him alive, in spite of his fearful squealing.

Every now and then bears take to killing cattle regularly. Sometimes the criminal is a female with cubs; sometimes an old male in spring, when he is lean, and has the flesh hunger upon him. But on one occasion a very large and cunning bear, some twenty-five miles below my ranch, took to cattle-killing early in the summer, and continued it through the fall. He made his home in a very densely wooded bottom; but he wandered far and wide, and I have myself frequently seen his great, half-human footprints leading along some narrow divide, or across some great plateau, where there was no cover whatever, and where he must have gone at night. During the daytime, when on one of these expeditions, he would lie up in some timber *coulee*, and return to the river-bottoms after dark, so that no one ever saw him; but his tracks were seen very frequently.

He began operations on the bottom where he had his den. He at first took to lying in wait for the cattle as they came down to drink, when he would seize some animal, usually a fat young steer or heifer, knocking it over by sheer force. In his furious rush he sometimes broke the back with a terrific blow from his fore-paw; at other times he threw the animal over and bit it to death. The rest of the herd never made any effort to retaliate, but fled in terror. Very soon the cattle would not go down on this bottom at all; then he began to wander over the adjoining bottoms, and finally to make excursions far off in the broken country. Evidently he would sometimes at night steal along a *coulee* until he found cattle lying down on the hillside, and then approach cautiously and seize his prey.

Usually the animals he killed were cows or steers; and noticing this, a certain ranchman in the neighborhood used to boast that a favorite bull on his ranch, of which he was particularly proud, would surely account for the bear if the latter dared to attack him. The boast proved vain. One day a cowboy riding down a lonely *coulee* came upon the scene of what had evidently been a very hard conflict. There were deep marks of hoofs and claws in the soft soil, bushes were smashed down where the struggling combatants had pressed against and over them, and a little farther on lay the remains of the bull.

He must have been seized by surprise; probably the great bear rushed at him from behind, or at one side, and fastened upon him so that he had no fair chance to use his horns. Nevertheless, he made a gallant struggle for his life, staggering to and fro trying to shake off his murderous antagonist, and endeavoring in vain to strike back over his shoulder; but all was useless. Even his strength could not avail against the might of his foe, and the cruel claws and teeth tore out his life. At last the gallant bull fell and breathed his last, and the bear feasted on the carcass.

The angry ranchman swore vengeance, and set a trap for the bear, hoping it would return. The sly old beast, however, doubtless was aware that the body had been visited, for he never came back, but returned to the river-bottom, and again from time to time was heard of as slaying some animal. However, at last his fate overtook him. Early one morning a cow was discovered just killed and not yet eaten, the bear having probably been scared off. Immediately the ranchman put poison in the bait which the bear had thus himself left, and twenty-four hours later the shaggy beast was found lying dead within a dozen yards of his last victim.

"Camp in the Forest," from *The Wilderness Hunter*.

A Black Bear Hunt in the Selkirks

Chapter V

When this interlude was over we resumed our march, toiling silently onwards through the wild and rugged country. Towards evening the valley widened a little, and we were able to walk in the bottoms, which much lightened our labor. The hunter, for greater ease, had tied the thongs of his heavy pack across his breast, so that he could not use his rifle; but my pack was lighter, and I carried it in a manner that would not interfere with my shooting, lest we should come unawares in game.

It was well that I did so. An hour or two before sunset we were travelling, as usual, in Indian file, beside the stream, through an open wood of great hemlock trees. There was no breeze, and we made no sound as we marched, for our feet sunk noiselessly into the deep sponge of moss, while the incessant dashing of the torrent, churning among the stones, would have drowned a far louder advance.

Suddenly the hunter, who was leading, dropped down in his tracks, pointing forward; and some fifty feet beyond I saw the head and shoulders of a bear as he rose to make a sweep at some berries. He was in a hollow where a tall, rank, prickly plant, with broad leaves, grew luxuriantly; and he was gathering its red berries, rising on his hind legs and sweeping them down into his mouth with his paw, and was much too intent on his work to notice us, for his head was pointed the other way. The moment he rose again I fired, meaning to shoot through the shoulders, but instead, in the hurry, taking him in the neck. Down he went, but whether hurt or not we could not see, for the second he was on all fours he was no longer visible. Rather to my surprise he uttered no sound—for bear when hit or when charging often make a great noise—so I raced forward to the edge of the hollow, the hunter close behind me, while Ammál danced about in the rear, very much excited, as Indians always are in the presence of big game. The instant we reached the hollow and looked down into it from the low bank on which we stood we saw by the swaying of the tall plants that the bear was coming our way. The hunter was standing some ten feet distant, a hemlock trunk being between us; and the next moment the bear sprang clean up the bank the other side of the hemlock, and almost within arm's length of my companion. I do not think he had intended to charge; he was probably confused by the bullet through his neck, and had by chance blundered out of the hollow in our direction; but when he saw the hunter so close he turned for him, his hair bristling and his teeth showing. The man had no cartridge in his weapon, and with his pack on could not have used it anyhow; and for a moment it looked as if he stood a fair chance of being hurt, though it is not likely that the bear would have done more than knock him down with his powerful forepaw, or perchance give him a single bite in passing. However, as the beast sprang out of the hollow he poised for a second on the edge of the bank to recover his balance, giving me a beautiful shot, as he stood sideways to me; the bullet struck between the eye and ear, and he fell as if hit with a pole axe.

Immediately the Indian began jumping about the body, uttering wild yells, his usually impassive face lit up with excitement, while the hunter and I stood at rest, leaning on our rifles and laughing. It was a strange scene, the dead bear lying in the shade of the giant hemlocks, while the fantastic-looking savage danced round him with shrill whoops, and the tall frontiersman looked quietly on.

Our prize was a large black bear, with two curious brown streaks down his back, one on each side the spine. We skinned him and camped by the carcass, as it was growing late. To take the chill off the evening air we built a huge fire, the logs roaring and crackling. To the side of it we made our beds—of balsam and hemlock boughs; we did not build a brush lean-to, because the night seemed likely to be clear. Then we supped on sugarless tea, frying-pan bread, and quantities of bear meat, fried or roasted—and how very good it tasted only those know who have gone through much hardship and some little hunger, and have worked violently for several days without flesh food. After eating our fill we stretched ourselves around the fire; the leaping sheets of flame lighted the tree-trunks round about, causing them to start out against the cavernous blackness beyond, and reddened the interlacing branches that formed a canopy overhead. The Indian sat on his haunches, gazing steadily and silently into the pile of blazing logs, while the white hunter and I talked together.

"Close Quarters with Old Ephraim," from *Hunting Trips of a Ranchman*.

Old
Ephraim
Chapter VI

But few bears are found in the immediate neighborhood of my ranch; and though I have once or twice seen their tracks in the Bad Lands, I have never had any experience with the animals themselves except during the elk-hunting trip on the Bighorn Mountains.

The grizzly bear undoubtedly comes in the category of dangerous game, and is, perhaps, the only animal in the United States that can be fairly so placed, unless we count the few jaguars found north of the Rio Grande. But the danger of hunting the grizzly has been greatly exaggerated, and the sport is certainly very much safer than it was at the beginning of this century. The first hunters who came into contact with this great bear were men belonging to that hardy and adventurous class of backwoodsmen which had filled the wild country between the Appalachian Mountains and the Mississippi. These men carried but one weapon: the long-barrelled, small-bored pea-rifle, whose bullets ran seventy to the pound, the amount of powder and lead being a litle less than that contained in the cartridge of a thirty-two calibre Winchester. In the eastern states almost all the hunting was done in the woodland; the shots were mostly obtained at short distance, and deer and black bear were the largest game; moreover, the pea-rifles were marvellously accurate for close range, and their owners were famed the world over for their skill as marksmen. Thus these rifles had so far proved plenty good enough for the work they had to to, and indeed had done excellent service as military weapons in the ferocious wars that the men of the border carried on with their Indian neighbors, and even in conflict with more civilized foes, as at the battles of Kings' Mountain and New Orleans. But when the restless frontiersmen pressed out over the Western plains, they encountered in the grizzly a beast of far greater bulk and more savage temper than any of those found in the Eastern woods, and their small-bore rifles were utterly inadequate weapons with which to cope with him. It is small wonder that he was considered by them to be almost invulnerable, and extraordinarily tenacious of life. He would be a most unpleasant antagonist now to a man armed only with a thirty-two calibre rifle that carried but a single shot and was loaded at the muzzle. A rifle, to be of use in this sport, should carry a ball weighing from half an ounce to an ounce. With the old pea-rifles the shot had to be in the eye or heart; and accidents to the hunter were very common. But the introduction of heavy breech-loading repeaters has greatly lessened the danger, even in the very few and far-off places where the grizzlies are as ferocious as formerly. For nowadays these great bears are undoubtedly much better aware of the death-dealing power of men, and, as a consequence, much less fierce, than was the case with their forefathers, who so unhesitatingly attacked the early Western travellers and explorers. Constant contact with rifle-carrying hunters, for a period extending over many generations of bear life, has taught the grizzly by bitter experience that man is his undoubted overlord, as far as fighting goes; and this knowledge has become an hereditary characteristic. No grizzly will assail a man now unprovoked, and one will almost always rather run than fight; though if he is wounded or thinks himself cornered he will attack his foes with a headlong, reckless fury that renders him one of the most dangerous of wild beasts. The ferocity of all wild animals depends largely upon the amount of resistance they are accustomed to meet with, and the quantity of molestation to which they are subjected.

The change in the grizzly's character during the last half century has been precisely paralleled by the change in the characters of its Northern cousin, the polar bear, and of the South African lion. When the Dutch and Scandinavian sailors first penetrated the Arctic seas, they were kept in constant dread of the white bear, who regarded a man as simply an erect variety of seal, quite as good eating as the common kind. The records of these early explorers are filled with examples of the ferocious and man-eating propensities of the polar bears; but in the accounts of most of the later Arctic expeditions, they are portrayed as having learned wisdom, and being now most anxious to keep out of the way of the hunters. A number of my sporting friends have killed white bears, and none of them were ever even charged. And in South Africa the English sportsmen and Dutch Boers have taught the lion to be a very different creature from what it was when the first white man reached that continent. If the Indian tiger had been a native of the United States, it would now be one of the most shy of beasts. Of late years our estimate of the grizzly's ferocity has been lowered; and we no longer accept the tales of uneducated hunters as being proper authority by which to judge it. But we should make a parallel reduction in the cases of many foreign animals and their describers. Take, for example, that purely melodramatic beast, the North African lion, as portrayed by Jules Gérard, who bombastically describes himself as *"le tueur des lions."* Gérard's accounts are self-evidently in large part fictitious, while, if true, they would prove less for the bravery of the lion than for the phenomenal cowardice, incapacity, and bad marksmanship of the Algerian Arabs. Doubtless Gérard was a great hunter; but so is many a Western plainsman, whose account of the grizzlies he has killed would be wholly untrustworthy. Take, for instance, the following from page 223 of *La Chasse au Lion:* "The inhabitants had assembled one day to the number of two or three hundred, with the object of killing (the lion) or driving it out of the country. The attack took place at sunrise; at midday five hundred cartridges had been expended; the Arabs carried off one of their number dead and six wounded, and the lion remained master of the field of battle." Now, if three hundred men could fire five hundred shots at a lion without hurting him, it merely shows that they were wholly incapable of hurting anything, or else that M. Gérard was more expert with the long-bow than with the rifle. Gérard's whole book is filled with equally preposterous nonsense; yet a great many people seriously accept this same book as trustworthy authority for the manners and ferocity of the North African lion. It would be quite as sensible to accept M. Jules Verne's stories as being valuable contributions to science. A good deal of the lion's reputation is built upon just such stuff.

How the prowess of the grizzly compares with that of the lion or tiger would be hard to say; I have never shot either of the latter myself, and my brother, who has killed tigers in India, has never had a chance at a grizzly. Any one of the big bears we killed on the mountains would, I should think, have been able to make short work of either a lion or a tiger; for the grizzly is greatly superior in bulk and muscular power to either of the great cats, and its teeth are as large as theirs, while its claws, though blunter, are much longer; nevertheless, I believe that a lion or a tiger would be fully as dangerous to a hunter or other human being, on account of the superior speed of its charge, the lightning-like rapidity of its movements, and its apparently sharper senses. Still, after all is said, the man should have a thoroughly trustworthy weapon and a fairly cool head, who would follow into its own haunts and slay grim Old Ephraim.

A grizzly will only fight if wounded or cornered, or, at least, if he thinks himself cornered. If a man by accident stumbles on to one close up, he's almost certain to be attacked really more from fear than from any other motive; exactly the same reason that makes a rattlesnake strike at a passer-by. I have personally known of but one instance of a grizzly turning on a hunter before being wounded. This happened to a friend of mine, a Californian ranchman, who, with two or three of his men, was following a bear that had carried off one of his sheep. They got the bear into a cleft in the mountain from which there was no escape, and he suddenly charged back through the line of his pursuers, struck down one of the horsemen, seized the arm of the man in his jaws and broke it as if it had been a pipe-stem, and was only killed after a most lively fight, in which, by repeated charges, he at one time drove every one of his assailants off the field.

But two instances have come to my personal knowledge where a man has been killed by a grizzly. One was that of a hunter at the foot of the Bighorn Mountains who had chased a large bear and finally wounded him. The animal turned at once and came straight at the man, whose second shot missed. The bear then closed and passed on, after striking only a single blow; yet that one blow, given with all the power of its thick, immensely muscular forearm, armed with nails as strong as so many hooked steel spikes, tore out the man's collar-bone and snapped through three or four ribs. He never recovered from the shock, and died that night.

The other instance occurred to a neighbor of mine—who has a small ranch on the Little Missouri—two or three years ago. He was out on a mining trip, and was prospecting with two other men near the headwater of the Little Missouri, in the Black Hills country. They were walking down along the river, and came to a point of land thrust out into it, which was densely covered with brush and fallen timber. Two of the party walked round by the edge of the stream; but the third, a German, and a very powerful fellow, followed a well-beaten game trail, leading through the bushy point. When they were some forty yards apart the two men heard an agonized shout from the German, and at the same time the loud coughing growl, or roar, of a bear. They turned just in time to see their compaion struck a terrible blow on the head by a grizzly, which must have been roused from its lair by his almost stepping on it; so close was it that he had no time to fire his rifle, but merely held it up over his head as a guard. Of course, it was struck down, the claws of the great brute at the same time shattering his skull like an egg-shell. Yet the man staggered on some ten feet before he fell; but when he did he never spoke or moved again. The two others killed the bear after a short brisk struggle as he was in the midst of a most determined charge.

In 1872, near Fort Wingate, New Mexico, two soldiers of a cavalry regiment came to their death at the claws of a grizzly bear. The army surgeon who attended them told me the particulars, as far as they were known. The men were mail-carriers, and one day did not come in at the appointed time. Next day a relief party was sent out to look for them, and after some search found the bodies of both, as well as that of one of the horses. One of the men still showed signs of life; he came to his senses before dying, and told the story. They had seen a grizzly, and pursued it on horseback with their Spencer rifles. On coming close, one had fired into its side, when it turned with marvellous quickness for so large and unwieldy an animal, and struck down the horse, at the same time inflicting a ghastly wound on the rider. The other man dismounted and came up to the rescue of his companion. The bear then left the latter and attacked the other. Although hit by the bullet, it charged home and threw the man down, and then lay on him and deliberately bit him to death, while his groans and cries were frightful to hear. Afterward it walked off into the bushes without again offering to molest the already mortally wounded victim of its first assault.

At certain times the grizzly works a good deal of havoc among the herds of the stockmen. A friend of mine, a ranchman in Montana, told me that one fall bears became very plenty around his ranches, and caused him severe loss, killing with ease even full-grown beef-steers. But one of them once found his intended quarry too much for him. My friend had a stocky, rather vicious range stallion, which had been grazing one day near a small thicket of bushes, and, towards evening, came galloping in with three or four gashes in his haunch, that looked as if they had been cut with a dull axe. The cowboys knew at once that he had been assailed by a bear, and rode off to the thicket near which he had been feeding. Sure enough, a bear, evidently in a very bad temper, sallied out as soon as the thicket was surrounded, and, after a spirited fight and a succession of charges, was killed. On examination, it was found that his under jaw was broken, and part of his face smashed in, evidently by the stallion's hoofs. The horse had been feeding when the bear leaped out at him, but failed to kill at the first stroke; then the horse lashed out behind, and not only freed himself, but also severely damaged his opponent.

Doubtless the grizzly could be hunted to advantage with dogs, which would not, of course, be expected to seize him, but simply to find and bay him, and distract his attention by barking and nipping. Occasionally, a bear can be caught in the open and killed with the aid of horses. But nine times out of ten the only way to get one is to put on moccasins and still-hunt it in its own haunts, shooting it at close quarters. Either its tracks should be followed until the bed wherein it lies during the day is found, or a given locality in which it is known to exist should be carefully beaten through, or else a bait should be left out, and a watch kept on it to catch the bear when he has come to visit it.

For some days after our arrival on the Bighorn range we did not come across any grizzly.

Although it was still early in September, the weather was cool and pleasant, the nights being frosty; and every two or three days there was a flurry of light snow, which rendered the labor of tracking much more easy. Indeed, throughout our stay on the mountains, the peaks were snow-capped almost all the time. Our fare was excellent, consisting of elk venison, mountain grouse, and small trout—the last caught in one of the beautiful little lakes that lay almost up by timber line. To us, who had for weeks been accustomed to make small fires from dried brush, or from sage-brush roots, which we dug out of the ground, it was a treat to sit at night before the roaring and crackling pine logs; as the old teamster quaintly put it, we had at last come to a land "where the wood grew on trees." There were plenty of black-tail deer in the woods, and we came across a number of bands of cow and calf elk, or of young bulls; but after several days' hunting we were still without any head worth taking home, and had seen no sign of grizzly, which was the game we were especially anxious to kill; for neither Merrifield nor I had ever seen a wild bear alive.

Sometimes we hunted in company; sometimes each of us went out alone; the teamster, of course, remaining in to guard camp and cook. One day we had separated; I reached camp early in the afternoon, and waited a couple of hours before Merrifield put in an appearance.

At last I heard a shout—the familiar long-drawn *Eikoh-h-h* of the cattlemen,—and he came in sight galloping at speed down an open glade, and waving his hat, evidently having had good luck; and when he reined in his small, wiry, cow-pony, we saw that he had packed behind his saddle the fine, glossy pelt of a black bear. Better still, he announced that he had been off about ten miles to a perfect tangle of ravines and valleys where bear sign was very thick; and not of black bear either, but of grizzly. The black bear (the only one we got on the mountains) he had run across by accident, while riding up a valley in which there was a patch of dead timber grown up with berry bushes. He noticed a black object which he first took to be a stump; for during the past few days we had each of us made one or two clever stalks up to charred logs, which our imagination converted into bears. On coming near, however, the object suddenly took to its heels; he followed over frightful ground at the pony's best pace, until it stumbled and fell down. By this time he was close on the bear, which had just reached the edge of the wood. Picking himself up, he rushed after it, hearing it growling ahead of him; after running some fifty yards the sound stopped, and he stood still listening. He saw and heard nothing, until he happened to cast his eyes upwards, and there was the bear, almost overhead, and about twenty-five feet up a tree; and in as many seconds afterwards it came down to the ground with a bounce, stone dead. It was a young bear, in its second year, and had probably never before seen a man, which accounted for the ease with which it was treed and taken. One minor result of the encounter was to convince Merrifield – the list of whose faults did not include lack of self-confidence – that he could run down any bear; in consequence of which idea we on more than one subsequent occasion went through a good deal of violent exertion.

Merrifield's tale made me decide to shift camp at once, and go over to the spot where the bear tracks were so plenty. Next morning we were off, and by noon pitched camp by a clear brook, in a valley with steep, wooded sides, but with good feed for the horses in the open bottom. We rigged the canvas wagon-sheet into a small tent, sheltered by the trees from the wind, and piled great pine logs near by where we wished to place the fire; for a night camp in the sharp fall weather is cold and dreary unless there is a roaring blaze of flame in front of the tent.

That afternoon we again went out, and I shot a fine bull elk. I came home alone toward nightfall, walking through a reach of burnt forest, where there was nothing but charred tree-trunks and black mould. When nearly through it I came across the huge, half-human footprints of a great grizzly, which must have passed by within a few minutes. It gave me rather an eerie feeling in the silent, lonely woods, to see for the first time the unmistakable proofs that I was in the home of the mighty lord of the wilderness. I followed the tracks in the fading twilight until it became too dark to see them any longer, and then shouldered my rifle and walked back to camp.

That evening we almost had a visit from one of the animals we were after. Several times we had heard at night the musical calling of the bull elk – a sound to which no writer has yet done justice. This particular night, when we were in bed and the fire was smouldering, we were roused by a ruder noise—a kind of grunting or roaring whine, answered by the frightened snorts of the ponies. It was a bear which had evidently not seen the fire, as it came from behind the bank, and had probably been attracted by the smell of the horses. After it made out what we were, it stayed round a short while, again uttered its peculiar roaring grunt, and went off; we had seized our rifles and had run out into the woods, but in the darkness could see nothing; indeed, it was rather lucky we did not stumble across the bear, as he could have made short work of us when we were at such a disadvantage.

Next day we went off on a long tramp through the woods and along the sides of the canyons. There were plenty of berry bushes growing in clusters; and all around these there were fresh tracks of bear. But the grizzly is also a flesh-eater, and has a great liking for carrion. On visiting the place where Merrifield had killed the black bear, we found that the grizzlies had been there before us, and had utterly devoured the carcass, with cannibal relish. Hardly a scrap was left, and we turned our steps toward where lay the bull elk I had killed. It was quite late in the afternoon when we reached the place. A grizzly had evidently been at the carcass during the preceding night, for his great footprints were in the ground all around it, and the carcass itself was gnawed and torn, and partially covered with earth and leaves—for the grizzly has a curious habit of burying all of his prey that he does not at the moment need. A great many ravens had been feeding on the body, and they wheeled about over the tree-tops above us, uttering their barking croaks.

The forest was composed mainly of what are called ridge-pole pines, which grow close together, and do not branch out until the stems are thirty or forty feet from the ground. Beneath these trees we walked over a carpet of pine needles, upon which our moccasined feet made no sound. The woods seemed vast and lonely, and their silence was broken now and then by the strange noises always to be heard in the great forests, and which seem to mark the sad and everlasting unrest of the wilderness. We climbed up along the trunk of a dead tree which had toppled over until its upper branches struck in the limb crotch of another, that thus supported it at an angle half way in its fall. When above the ground far enough to prevent the bear's smelling us, we sat still to wait for his approach; until, in the gathering gloom, we could no longer see the sights of our rifles, and could but dimly make out the carcass of the great elk. It was useless to wait longer; and we clambered down and stole out to the edge of the woods. The forest here covered one side of a steep, almost canyon-like ravine, whose other side was bare except of rock and sage-brush. Once out from under the trees there was still plenty of light, although the sun had set, and we crossed over some fifty yards to the opposite hillside, and crouched down under a bush to see if, perchance, some animal might not also leave the cover. To our right the ravine sloped downward toward the valley of the Bighorn River, and far on its other side we could catch a glimpse of the great main chain of the Rockies, their snow-peaks glinting crimson in the light of the set sun. Again we waited quietly in the growing dusk until the pine trees in our front blended into one dark, frowning mass. We saw nothing; but the wild creatures of the forest had begun to stir abroad. The owls hooted dismally from the tops of the tall trees, and two or three times a harsh wailing cry, probably the voice of some lynx or wolverine, arose from the depths of the woods. At last, as we were rising to leave, we heard the sound of the breaking of a dead stick from the spot where we knew the carcass lay. It was a sharp, sudden noise, perfectly distinct from the natural creaking and snapping of the branches; just such a sound as would be made by the tread of some heavy creature. "Old Ephraim" had come back to the carcass. A minute afterward, listening with strained ears, we heard him brush by some dry twigs. It was entirely too dark to go in after him; but we made up our minds that on the morrow he should be ours.

Early next morning we were over at the elk carcass, and, as we expected, found that the bear had eaten his full at it during the night. His tracks showed him to be an immense fellow, and were so fresh that we doubted if he had left long before we arrived; and we made up our minds to follow him up and try to find his lair. The bears that lived on these mountains had evidently been little disturbed; indeed, the Indians and most of the white hunters are rather chary of meddling with "Old Ephraim," as the mountain men style the grizzly, unless they get him at a disadvantage; for the sport is fraught with some danger and but small profit. The bears thus seemed to have very little fear of harm, and we thought it likely that the bed of the one who had fed on the elk would not be far away.

My companion was a skilful tracker, and we took up the trail at once. For some distance it led over the soft, yielding carpet of moss and pine needles, and the footprints were quite easily made out, although we could follow them but slowly; for we had, of course, to keep a sharp lookout ahead and around us as we walked noiselessly on in the sombre half-light always prevailing under the great pine trees, through whose thickly interlacing branches stray but few beams of light, no matter how bright the sun may be outside. We made no sound ourselves, and every little sudden noise sent a thrill through me as I peered about with each

"Head of Grizzly Bear shot September 13, 1884," from *Hunting Trips of a Ranchman*.

sense on the alert. Two or three of the ravens that we had scared from the carcass flew overhead, croaking hoarsely; and the pine-tops moaned and sighed in the slight breeze—for pine trees seem to be ever in motion, no matter how light the wind.

After going a few hundred yards the tracks turned off on a well-beaten path made by the elk; the woods were in many places cut up by these game trails, which had often become as distinct as ordinary foot-paths. The beast's footprints were perfectly plain in the dust, and he had lumbered along up the path until near the middle of the hillside, where the ground broke away, and there were hollows and boulders. Here there had been a windfall, and the dead trees lay among the living, piled across one another in all directions; while between and around them sprouted up a thick growth of young spruces and other evergreens. The trail turned off into the tangled thicket, within which it was almost certain we would find our quarry. We could still follow the tracks, by the slight scrapes of the claws on the bark, or by the bent and broken twigs; and we advanced with noiseless caution, slowly climbing over the dead tree trunks and upturned stumps, and not letting a branch rustle or catch on our clothes. When in the middle of the thicket we crossed what was almost a breast-work of fallen logs, and Merrifield, who was leading, passed by the upright stem of a great pine. As soon as he was by it, he sank suddenly on one knee, turning half round, his face fairly aflame with excitement; and as I strode past him, with my rifle at the ready, there, not ten steps off, was the great bear, slowly rising from his bed among the young spruces. He had heard us, but apparently hardly knew exactly where or what we were, for he reared up on his haunches sideways to us. Then he saw us, and dropped down again on all fours, the shaggy hair on his neck and shoulders seeming to bristle as he turned towards us. As he sank down on his forefeet I had raised the rifle; his head was bent slightly down, and when I saw the top of the white bead fairly between his small, glittering, evil eyes, I pulled trigger. Half rising up, the huge beast fell over on his side in the death throes, the ball having gone into his brain, striking as fairly between the eyes as if the distance had been measured by a carpenter's rule.

The whole thing was over in twenty seconds from the time I caught sight of the game; indeed, it was over so quickly that the grizzly did not have time to show fight at all or come a step toward us. It was the first I had ever seen, and I felt not a little proud, as I stood over the great brindled bulk, which lay stretched out at length in the cool shade of the evergreens. He was a monstrous fellow, much larger than any I have seen since, whether alive or brought in dead by the hunters. As near as we could estimate (for of course we had nothing with which to weigh more than very small portions) he must have weighed about twelve hundred pounds, and though this is not as large as some of his kind are said to grow in California, it is yet a very unusual size for a bear. He was a good deal heavier than any of our horses; and it was with the greatest difficulty that we were able to skin him. He must have been very old, his teeth and claws being all worn down and blunted; but nevertheless he had been living in plenty, for he was as fat as a prize hog, the layers on his back being a finger's length in thickness. He was still in the summer coat, his hair being short, and in color a curious brindled brown, somewhat like that of certain bulldogs; while all the bears we shot afterward had the long thick winter fur, cinnamon or yellowish brown. By the way, the name of this bear has reference to its character and not to its color, and should, I suppose, be properly spelt grisly—in the sense of horrible, exactly as we speak of a "grisly spectre"—and not grizzly; but perhaps the latter way of spelling it is too well established to be now changed.

In killing dangerous game, steadiness is more needed than good shooting. No game is dangerous unless a man is close up, for nowadays hardly any wild beast will charge from a distance of a hundred yards, but will rather try to run off; and if a man is close it is easy enough for him to shoot straight if he does not lose his head. A bear's brain is about the size of a pint bottle; and any one can hit a pint bottle offhand at thirty or forty feet. I have had two shots at bears at close quarters, and each time I fired into the brain, the bullet in one case striking fairly between the eyes, as told above, and in the other going in between the eye and ear. A novice at this kind of sport will find it best and safest to keep in mind the old Norse viking's advice in reference to a long sword: "If you go in close enough your sword will be long enough." If a poor shot goes in close enough he will find that he shoots straight enough.

I was very proud over my first bear; but Merrifield's chief feeling seemed to be disappointment that the animal had not had time to show fight. He was rather a reckless fellow, and very confident in his own skill with the rifle; and he really did not seem to have any more fear of the grizzlies than if they had been so many jack-rabbits. I did not at all share his feelings, having a hearty respect for my foes' prowess, and in following and attacking them always took all possible care to get the chances on my side. Merrifield was sincerely sorry that we never had to stand a regular charge; while on this trip we killed five grizzlies with seven bullets, and, except in the case of the she and cub spoken of farther on, each was shot about as quickly as it got sight of us. The last one we got was an old male, which was feeding on an elk carcass. We crept up to within about sixty feet, and as Merrifield had not yet killed a grizzly purely to his own gun, and I had killed three, I told him to take the shot. He at once whispered gleefully: "I'll break his leg, and we'll see what he'll do!" Having no ambition to be a participator in the antics of a three-legged bear, I hastily interposed a most emphatic veto; and with a rather injured air he fired, the bullet going through the neck just back of the head. The bear fell to the shot, and could not get up from the ground, dying in a few minutes; but first he seized his left wrist in his teeth and bit clean through it, completely separating the bones of the paw and arm. Although a smaller bear than the big one I first shot, he would probably have proved a much more ugly foe, for he was less unwieldy, and had much longer and sharper teeth and claws. I think that if my companion had merely broken the beast's leg, he would have had his curiosity as to its probable conduct more than gratified.

We tried eating the grizzly's flesh, but it was not good, being coarse and not well flavored; and besides, we could not get over the feeling that it had belonged to a carrion feeder. The flesh of the little black bear, on the other hand, was excellent; it tasted like that of a young pig. Doubtless, if a young grizzly, which had fed merely upon fruits, berries, and acorns, was killed, its flesh would prove good eating; but even then it would probably not be equal to a black bear.

A day or two after the death of the big bear, we went out one afternoon on horseback, intending merely to ride down to see a great canyon lying some six miles west of our camp; indeed, we went more to look at the scenery than for any other reason, though, of course, neither of us ever stirred out of camp without his rifle. We rode down the valley in which we had camped, through alternate pine groves and open glades, until we reached the canyon, and then skirted its brink for a mile or so. It was a great chasm, many miles in length, as if the table-land had been rent asunder by some terrible and unknown force; its sides were sheer walls of rock, rising three or four hundred feet straight up in the air, and worn by the weather till they looked like towers and battlements of some vast fortress. Between them, at the bottom, was a space, in some places nearly a quarter of a mile wide, in others very narrow, through whose middle foamed a deep, rapid torrent, of which the sources lay far back among the snow-topped mountains around Cloud Peak. In this valley, dark green sombre pines stood in groups, stiff and erect; and here and there among them were groves of poplar and cottonwood, with slender branches and trembling leaves, their bright green already changing to yellow in the sharp fall weather. We went down to where the mouth of the canyon opened out, and rode our horses to the end of a great jutting promontory of rock, thrust out into the plain; and in the cold, clear air we looked far over the broad valley of the Bighorn as it lay at our very feet, walled in on the other side by the distant chain of the Rocky Mountains.

Turning our horses, we rode back along the edge of another canyon-like valley, with a brook flowing down its center, and its rocky sides covered with an uninterrupted pine forest—the place of all others in whose inaccessible wildness and ruggedness a bear would find a safe retreat. After some time we came to where other valleys, with steep, grass-grown sides, covered with sage-brush, branched out from it, and we followed one of these out. There was plenty of elk sign about, and we saw several black-tail deer. These last were very common on the mountains, but we had not hunted them at all, as we were in no need of meat. But this afternoon we came across a buck with remarkably fine antlers, and accordingly I shot it, and we stopped to cut off and skin out the horns, throwing the reins over the heads of the horses, and leaving them to graze by themselves. The body lay near the crest of one side of a deep valley, or ravine, which headed up on the plateau a mile to our left. Except for scattered trees and bushes the valley was bare; but there was heavy timber along the crests of the hills on its opposite side. It took some time to fix the head properly, and we were just ending when Merrifield sprang to his feet and exclaimed: "Look at the bears!" pointing down into the valley below us. Sure enough, there were two bears (which afterwards proved to be an old she and a nearly full-grown cub) travelling up the bottom of the valley, much too far off for us to shoot. Grasping our rifles and throwing off our hats, we started off as hard as we could run, diagonally down the hillside, so as to cut them off. It was some little time before they saw us, when they made off at a lumbering gallop up the valley. It would seem impossible to run into two grizzlies in the open, but they were going up hill and we down, and, moreover, the old one kept stopping. The cub would forge ahead and could probably have escaped us, but the mother now and then stopped to sit up on her haunches and look round at us, when the cub would run back to her. The upshot was that we got ahead of them, when they turned and went straight up one hillside as we ran straight down the other behind them. By this time I was pretty nearly done out, for running along the steep ground through the sage-brush was most exhausting work; and Merrifield kept gaining on me and was well in front. Just as he disappeared over a bank, almost at the bottom of the valley, I tripped over a bush and fell full-length. When I got up I knew I could never make up the ground I had lost, and, besides, could hardly run any longer; Merrifield was out of sight below, and the bears were laboring up the steep hillside directly opposite and about three hundred yards off, so I sat down and began to shoot over Merrifield's head, aiming at the big bear. She was going very steadily and in a straight line, and each bullet sent up a puff of dust where it struck the dry soil, so that I could keep correcting my aim; and the fourth ball crashed into the old bear's flank. She lurched heavily forward, but recovered herself and reached the timber, while Merrifield, who had put on a spurt, was not far behind.

I toiled up the hill at a sort of trot, fairly gasping and sobbing for breath; but before I got to the top I heard a couple of shots and a shout. The old bear had turned as soon as she was in the timber, and came towards Merrifield, but he gave her the death wound by firing into her chest, and then shot at the young one, knocking it over. When I came up he was just walking toward the latter to finish it with the revolver, but it suddenly jumped up as lively as ever and made off at a great pace—for it was nearly full-grown. It was impossible to fire where the tree trunks were so thick, but there was a small opening across which it would have to pass, and, collecting all my energies, I made a last run, got into position, and covered the opening with my rifle. The instant the bear appeared I fired, and it turned a dozen somersaults down hill, rolling over and over; the ball had struck it near the tail, and had ranged forward through the hollow of the body. Each of us had thus given the fatal wound to the bear into which the other had fired the first bullet. The run, though short, had been very sharp, and over such awful country that we were completely fagged out, and could hardly speak for lack of breath. The sun had already set, and it was too late to skin the animals; so we merely dressed them, caught the ponies,—with some trouble, for they were frightened at the smell of the bear's blood on our hands,—and rode home through the darkening woods. Next day we brought the teamster and two of the steadiest pack-horses to the carcasses, and took the skins into camp.

The feed for the horses was excellent in the valley in which we were camped, and the rest after their long journey across the plains did them good. They had picked up wonderfully in condition during our stay on the mountains; but they were apt to wander very far during the night, for there were so many bears and other wild beasts around, that they kept getting frightened and running off. We were very loath to leave our hunting-grounds, but time was pressing, and we had already many more trophies than we could carry; so one cool morning, when the branches of the evergreens were laden with the feathery snow that had fallen overnight, we struck camp and started out of the mountains, each of us taking his own bedding behind his saddle, while the pack-horses were loaded down with bearskins, elk and deer antlers, and the hides and furs of other game. In single file we moved through the woods, and across the canyons to the edge of the great table-land, and then slowly down the steep slope to its foot, where we found our canvas-topped wagon; and next day saw us setting out on our long journey homewards, across the three hundred weary miles of treeless and barren-looking plains country.

Last spring, since the above was written, a bear killed a man not very far from my ranch. It was at the time of the floods. Two hunters came down the river, by our ranch, on a raft, stopping to take dinner. A score or so of miles below, as we afterwards heard from the survivor, they landed, and found a bear in a small patch of brushwood. After waiting in vain for it to come out, one of the men rashly attempted to enter the thicket, and was instantly struck down by the beast, before he could so much as fire his rifle. It broke in his skull with a blow of its great paw, and then seized his arm in its jaws, biting it through and through in three places, but leaving the body and retreating into the bushes as soon as the unfortunate man's companion approached. We did not hear of the accident until too late to go after the bear, as we were just about starting to join the spring round-up.

"The Death of the Grizzly," from *The Wilderness Hunter*.

Hunting
the
Grizzly
Chapter VII

If out in the late fall or early spring, it is often possible to follow a bear's trail in the snow; having come upon it either by chance or hard hunting, or else having found where it leads from some carcass on which the beast has been feeding. In the pursuit one must exercise great caution, as at such times the hunter is easily seen a long way off, and game is always especially watchful for any foe that may follow its trail.

Once I killed a grizzly in this manner. It was early in the fall, but snow lay on the ground, while the gray weather boded a storm. My camp was in a bleak, wind-swept valley, high among the mountains which form the divide between the head-waters of the Salmon and Clark's Fork of the Columbia. All night I had lain in my buffalo-bag, under the lea of a windbreak of branches, in the clump of fir-trees, where I had halted the preceding evening. At my feet ran a rapid mountain torrent, its bed choked with ice-covered rocks; I had been lulled to sleep by the stream's splashing murmur, and the loud moaning of the wind along the naked cliffs. At dawn I rose and shook myself free of the buffalo robe, coated with hoar-frost. The ashes of the fire were lifeless; in the dim morning the air was bitter cold. I did not linger a moment, but snatched up my rifle, pulled on my fur cap and gloves, and strode off up a side ravine; as I walked I ate some mouthfuls of venison, left over from supper.

Two hours of toil up the steep mountain brought me to the top of a spur. The sun had risen, but was hidden behind a bank of sullen clouds. On the divide I halted, and gazed out over a vast landscape, inconceivably wild and dismal. Around me towered the stupendous mountain masses which make up the backbone of the Rockies. From my feet, as far as I could see, stretched a rugged and barren chaos of ridges and detached rock masses. Behind me, far below, the stream wound like a silver ribbon, fringed with dark conifers and the changing, dying foliage of poplar and quaking aspen. In front the bottoms of the valleys were filled with the sombre evergreen forest, dotted here and there with black, ice-skimmed tarns; and the dark spruces clustered also in the higher gorges, and were scattered thinly along the mountain sides. The snow which had fallen lay in drifts and streaks, while, where the wind had scope it was blown off, and the ground left bare.

For two hours I walked onwards across the ridges and valleys. Then among some scattered spruces, where the snow lay to the depth of half a foot, I suddenly came on the fresh, broad trail of a grizzly. The brute was evidently roaming restlessly about in search of a winter den, but willing, in passing, to pick up any food that lay handy. At once I took the trail, travelling above and to one side, and keeping a sharp look-out ahead. The bear was going across wind, and this made my task easy. I walked rapidly, though cautiously; and it was only in crossing the large patches of bare ground that I had to fear making a noise. Elsewhere the snow muffled my footsteps, and made the trail so plain that I scarcely had to waste a glance upon it, bending my eyes always to the front.

At last, peering cautiously over a ridge crowned with broken rocks, I saw my quarry, a big, burly bear, with silvered fur. He had halted on an open hill-side, and was busily digging up the caches of some rock gophers or squirrels. He seemed absorbed in his work, and the stalk was easy. Slipping quietly back, I ran towards the end of the spur, and in ten minutes struck a ravine, of which one branch ran past within seventy yards of where the bear was working. In this ravine was a rather close growth of stunted evergreens, affording good cover, although in one or two places I had to lie down and crawl through the snow. When I reached the point for which I was aiming, the bear had just finished rooting, and was starting off. A slight whistle brought him to a standstill, and I drew a bead behind his shoulder, and low down, resting the rifle across the crooked branch of a dwarf spruce. At the crack he ran off at speed, making no sound, but the thick spatter of blood splashes, showing clear on the white snow, betrayed the mortal nature of the wound. For some minutes I followed the trail; and when, topping a ridge, I saw the dark bulk lying motionless in a snow drift at the foot of a low rock-wall, down which he had tumbled.

The usual practice of the still-hunter who is after grizzly is to toll it to baits. The hunter either lies in ambush near the carcass, or approaches it stealthily when he thinks the bear is at its meal.

One day while camped near the Bitter Root Mountains in Montana I found that a bear had been feeding on the carcass of a moose which lay some five miles from the little open glade in which my tent was pitched, and I made up my mind to try to get a shot at it that afternoon. I stayed in camp till about three o'clock, lying lazily back on the bed of sweet-smelling evergreen boughs, watching the pack ponies as they stood under the pines on the edge of the open, stamping now and then, and switching their tails. The air was still, the sky a glorious blue; at that hour in the afternoon even the September sun was hot. The smoke from the smouldering logs of the camp fire curled thinly upwards. Little chipmunks scuttled out from their holes to the packs, which lay in a heap on the ground, and then scuttled madly back again. A couple of drab-colored whiskey-jacks, with bold mien and fearless bright eyes, hopped and fluttered round, picking up the scraps, and uttering an extraordinary variety of notes, mostly discordant; so tame were they that one of them lit on my outstretched arm as I half dozed, basking in the sunshine.

When the shadows began to lengthen, I shouldered my rifle and plunged into the woods. At first my route lay along a mountain side; then for half a mile over a windfall, the dead timber piled about in crazy confusion. After that I went up the bottom of a valley by a little brook, the ground being carpeted with a sponge of soaked moss. At the head of this brook was a pond covered with water-lilies; and a scramble through a rocky pass took me into a high, wet valley, where the thick growth of spruce was broken by occasional strips of meadow. In this valley the moose carcass lay, well at the upper end.

In moccasined feet I trod softly through the soundless woods. Under the dark branches it was already dusk, and the air had the cool chill of evening. As I neared the clump where the body lay, I walked with redoubled caution, watching and listening with strained alertness. Then I heard a twig snap; and my blood leaped, for I knew the bear was at his supper. In another moment I saw his shaggy, brown form. He was working with all his awkward giant strength, trying to bury the carcass, twisting it to one side and the other with wonderful ease. Once he got angry and suddenly gave it a tremendous cuff with his paw; in his bearing he had something half humorous, half devilish. I crept up within forty yards; but for several minutes he would not keep his head still. Then something attracted his attention in the forest, and he stood motionless looking towards it, broadside to me, with his fore-paws planted on the carcass. This gave me my chance. I drew a very fine bead between his eye and ear, and pulled the trigger. He dropped like a steer when struck with a pole-axe.

If there is a good hiding place handy it is better to lie in wait at the carcass. One day on the head-waters of the Madison, I found that a bear was coming to an elk I had shot some days before; and I at once determined to ambush the beast when he came back that evening. The carcass lay in the middle of a valley a quarter of a mile broad. The bottom of this valley was covered by an open forest of tall pines; a thick jungle of smaller evergreens marked where the mountains rose on either hand. There were a number of large rocks scattered here and there, one, of very convenient shape, being only some seventy or eighty yards from the carcass. Up this I clambered. It hid me perfectly, and on its top was a carpet of soft pine needles, on which I could lie at my ease.

Hour after hour passed by. A little black woodpecker with a yellow crest ran nimbly up and down the tree trunks for some time and then flitted away with a party of chickadees and nut-hatches. Occasionally a Clark's crow soared about overhead or clung in any position to the swaying end of a pine branch, chattering and screaming. Flocks of crossbills, with wavy flight and plaintive calls, flew to a small mineral lick near by, where they scraped the clay with their queer little beaks.

As the westering sun sank out of sight beyond the mountains these sounds of bird-life gradually died away. Under the great pines the evening was still with the silence of primeval desolation. The sense of sadness and loneliness, the melancholy of the wilderness, came over me like a spell. Every slight noise made my pulses throb as I lay motionless on the rock gazing intently into the gathering gloom. I began to fear that it would grow too dark to shoot before the grizzly came.

Suddenly and without warning, the great bear stepped out of the bushes and trod across the pine needles with such swift and silent footsteps that its bulk seemed unreal. It was very cautious, continually halting to peer around; and once it stood up on its hind legs and I looked long down the valley towards the red west. As it reached the carcass I put a bullet between its shoulders. It rolled over, while the woods resounded with its savage roaring. Immediately it struggled to its feet and staggered off; and fell again to the next shot, squalling and yelling. Twice this was repeated; the brute being one of those bears which greet every wound with a great outcry, and sometimes seem to lose their feet when hit—although they will occasionally fight as savagely as their more silent brethren. In this case the wounds were mortal, and the bear died before reaching the edge of the thicket.

I spent much of the fall of 1889 hunting on the head-waters of the Salmon and Snake in Idaho, and along the Montana boundary line from the Big Hole Basin and the head of the Wisdom River to the neighborhood of Red Rock Pass and to the north and west of Henry's Lake. During the last fortnight my companion was the old mountain man, already mentioned, named Griffeth or Griffin—I cannot tell which, as he was always called either "Hank" or "Griff." He was a crabbedly honest old fellow, and a very skilful hunter; but he was worn out with age and rheumatism, and his temper had failed even faster than his bodily strength. He showed me a greater variety of game than I had ever seen before in so short a time; nor did I ever before or after make so successful a hunt. But he was an exceedingly disagreeable companion on account of his surly, moody ways. I generally had to get up first, to kindle the fire and make ready breakfast, and he was very quarrelsome. Finally, during my absence from camp one day, while not very far from Red Rock Pass, he found my whiskey flask, which I kept purely for emergencies, and drank all the contents. When I came back he was quite drunk. This was unbearable, and after some high words I left him, and struck off homeward through the woods on my own account. We had with us four pack and saddle horses; and of these I took a very intelligent and gentle little bronco mare, which possessed the invaluable trait of always staying near camp, even when not hobbled. I was not hampered with much of an outfit, having only my buffalo sleeping-bag, a fur coat, and my washing kit, with a couple of spare pairs of socks and some handkerchiefs. A frying-pan, some salt, flour, baking-powder, a small chunk of salt pork, and a hatchet, made up a light pack, which, with the bedding, I fastened across the stock saddle by means of a rope and a spare packing cinch. My cartridges and knife were in my belt; my compass and matches, as always, in my pocket. I walked, while the little mare followed almost like a dog, often without my having to hold the lariat which served as halter.

The country was for the most part fairly open, as I kept near the foothills where glades and little prairies broke the pine forest. The trees were of small size. There was no regular trail, but the course was easy to keep, and I had no trouble of any kind save on the second day. That afternoon I was following a stream which at last "canyoned up," that is, sank to the bottom of a canyon-like ravine impassable for a horse. I started up a side valley, intending to cross from its head coulies to those of another valley which would lead in below the canyon.

However, I got enmeshed in the tangle of winding valleys at the foot of the steep mountains, and as dusk was coming on I halted and camped in a little open spot by the side of a small, noisy brook, with crystal water. The place was carpeted with soft, wet, green moss, dotted red with the kinnikinnic berries, and at its edge, under the trees where the ground was dry, I threw down the buffalo bed on the mat of sweet-smelling pine needles. Making camp took but a moment. I opened the pack, tossed the bedding on a smooth spot, knee-haltered the little mare, dragged up a few dry logs, and then strolled off, rifle on shoulder, through the frosty gloaming, to see if I could pick up a grouse for supper.

For half a mile I walked quickly and silently over the pine needles, across a succession of slight ridges separated by narrow, shallow valleys. The forest here was composed of lodgepole pines, which on the ridges grew close together, with tall slender trunks, while in the valleys the growth was more open. Though the sun was behind the mountains there was yet plenty of light by which to shoot, but it was fading rapidly.

At last, as I was thinking of turning towards camp, I stole up to the crest of one of the ridges, and looked over into the valley some sixty yards off. Immediately I caught the loom of some large, dark object; and another glance showed me a big grizzly walking slowly off with his head down. He was quartering to me, and I fired into his flank, the bullet, as I afterwards found, ranging forward and piercing one lung. At the shot he uttered a loud, moaning grunt and plunged forward at a heavy gallop, while I raced obliquely down the hill to cut him off. After going a few hundred feet he reached a laurel thicket, some thirty yards broad, and two or three times as long which he did not leave. I ran up to the edge and there halted, not liking to venture into the mass of twisted, close-growing stems and glossy foliage. Moreover, as I halted, I heard him utter a peculiar, savage kind of whine from the heart of the brush. Accordingly, I began to skirt the edge, standing on tiptoe and gazing earnestly to see if I could not catch a glimpse of his hide. When I was at the narrowest part of the thicket, he suddenly left it directly opposite, and then wheeled and stood broadside to me on the hill-side, a little above. He turned his head stiffly towards me; scarlet strings of froth hung from his lips; his eyes burned like embers in the gloom.

I held true, aiming behind the shoulder, and my bullet shattered the point or lower end of his heart, taking out a big nick. Instantly the great bear turned with a harsh roar of fury and challenge, blowing the bloody foam from his mouth, so that I saw the gleam of his white fangs; and then he charged straight at me, crashing and bounding through the laurel bushes, so that it was hard to aim. I waited until he came to a fallen tree, raking him as he topped it with a ball, which entered his chest and went through the cavity of his body, but he neither swerved nor flinched, and at the moment I did not know that I had struck him. He came steadily on, and in another second was almost upon me. I fired for his forehead, but my bullet went low, entering his open mouth, smashing his lower jaw and going into the neck. I leaped to one side almost as I pulled the trigger; and through the hanging smoke the first thing I saw was his paw as he made a vicious side blow at me. The rush of his charge carried him past. As he struck he lurched forward, leaving a pool of bright blood where his muzzle hit the ground; but he recovered himself and made two or three jumps onwards, while I hurriedly jammed a couple of cartridges into the magazine, my rifle holding only four, all of which I had tried. Then he tried to pull up, but as he did so his muscles seemed suddenly to give way, his head drooped, and he rolled over and over like a shot rabbit. Each of my first three bullets had inflicted a mortal wound.

It was already twilight, and I merely opened the carcass, and then trotted back to camp. Next morning I returned and with much labor took off the skin. The fur was very fine, the animal being in excellent trim, and unusually bright-colored. Unfortunately, in packing it out I lost the skull, and had to supply its place with one of plaster. The beauty of the trophy, and the memory of the circumstances under which I procured it, make me value it perhaps more highly than any other in my house.

This is the only instance in which I have been regularly charged by a grizzly. On the whole, the danger of hunting these great bears has been much exaggerated. At the beginning of the present century, when white hunters first encountered the grizzly, he was doubtless an exceedingly savage beast, prone to attack without provocation, and a redoubtable foe to persons armed with the clumsy, small-bore, muzzle-loading rifles of the day. But at present bitter experience has taught him caution. He has been hunted for sport, and hunted for his pelt, and hunted for the bounty, and hunted as a dangerous enemy to stock, until, save in the very wildest districts, he has learned to be more wary than a deer, and to avoid man's presence almost as carefully as the most timid kind of game. Except in rare cases he will not attack of his own accord, and, as a rule, even when wounded his object is escape rather than battle.

Still, when fairly brought to bay, or when moved by a sudden fit of ungovernable anger, the grizzly is beyond peradventure a very dangerous antagonist. The first shot, if taken at a bear a good distance off and previously unwounded and unharried, is not usually fraught with much danger, the startled animal being at the outset bent merely on flight. It is always hazardous, however, to track a wounded and worried grizzly into thick cover, and the man who habitually follows and kills this chief of American game in dense timber, never abandoning the bloody trail whithersoever it leads, must show no small degree of skill and hardihood, and must not too closely count the risk to life or limb. Bears differ widely in temper, and occasionally one may be found who will not show fight, no matter how much he is bullied; but, as a rule, a hunter must be cautious in meddling with a wounded animal which has retreated into a dense thicket, and has been once or twice roused; and such a beast, when it does turn, will usually charge again and again, and fight to the last with unconquerable ferocity. The short distance at which the bear can be seen through the underbrush, the fury of his charge, and his tenacity of life make it necessary for the hunter on such occasions to have steady nerves and a fairly quick and accurate aim. It is always well to have two men in following a wounded bear under such conditions. This is not necessary, however, and a good hunter, rather than lose his quarry, will, under ordinary circumstances, follow and attack it no matter how tangled the fastness in which it has sought refuge; but he must act warily and with the utmost caution and resolution, if he wishes to escape a terrible and probably fatal mauling. An experienced hunter is rarely rash, and never heedless; he will not, when alone, follow a wounded bear into a thicket, if by the exercise of patience, skill, and knowledge of the game's habits he can avoid the necessity; but it is idle to talk of the feat as something which ought in no case to be attempted. While danger ought never to be needlessly incurred, it is yet true that the keenest zest in sport comes from its presence, and from the consequent exercise of the qualities necessary to overcome it. The most thrilling moments of an American hunter's life are those in which, with every sense on the alert, and with nerves strung to the highest point, he is following alone into the heart of its forest fastness the fresh and bloody footprints of an angered grizzly; and no other triumph of American hunting can compare with the victory to be thus gained.

These big bears will not ordinarily charge from a distance of over a hundred yards; but there are exceptions to this rule. In the fall of 1890 my friend Archibald Rogers was hunting in Wyoming, south of the Yellowstone Park, and killed seven bears. One, an old he, was out on a bare table-land, grubbing for roots, when he was spied. It was early in the afternoon, and the hunters, who were on a high mountain slope, examined him for some time through their powerful glasses before making him out to be a bear. They then stalked up to the edge of the wood which fringed the table-land on one side, but could get no nearer than about three hundred yards, the plains being barren of all cover. After waiting for a couple of hours Rogers risked the shot, in despair of getting nearer, and wounded the bear, though not very seriously. The animal made off, almost broadside to, and Rogers ran forward to intercept it. As soon as it saw him it turned and rushed straight for him, not heeding his second shot, and evidently bent on charging home. Rogers then waited until it was within twenty yards, and brained it with his third bullet.

In fact bears differ individually in courage and ferocity precisely as men do, or as the Spanish bulls, of which it is said that not more than one in twenty is fit to stand the combat of the arena. One grizzly can scarcely be bullied into resistance; the next may fight to the end, against any odds, without flinching, or even attack unprovoked. Hence men of limited experience in this sport, generalizing from the actions of the two or three bears each has happened to see or kill, often reach diametrically opposite conclusions as to the fighting temper and capacity of the quarry. Even old hunters—who indeed, as a class, are very narrow-minded and opinionated—often generalize just as rashly as beginners. One will portray all bears as very dangerous; another will speak and act as if he deemed them of no more consequence than so many rabbits. I knew one old hunter who had killed a score without ever seeing one show fight. On the other hand, Dr. James C. Merrill, U.S.A., who has had about as much experience with bears as I have had, informs me that he has been charged with the utmost determination three times. In each case the attack was delivered before the bear was wounded or even shot at, the animal being roused by the approach of the hunters from his day bed, and charging headlong at them from a distance of twenty or thirty paces. All three bears were killed before they could do any damage. There was a very remarkable incident connected with the killing of one of them. It occurred in the northern spurs of the Bighorn range. Dr. Merrill, in company with an old hunter, had climbed down into a deep, narrow canyon. The bottom was threaded with well-beaten elk trails. While following one of these the two men turned a corner of the canyon and were instantly charged by an old she-grizzly, so close that it was only by good luck that one of the hurried shots disabled her and caused her to tumble over a cut bank where she was easily finished. They found that she had been lying directly across the game trail, on a smooth well beaten patch of bare earth, which looked as if it had been dug up, refilled, and trampled down. Looking curiously at this patch they saw a bit of hide only partially covered at one end; digging down they found the body of a well grown grizzly cub. Its skull had been crushed, and the brains licked out, and there were signs of other injuries. The hunters pondered long over this strange discovery, and hazarded many guesses as to its meaning. At last they decided that probably the cub had been killed, and its brains eaten out, either by some old male-grizzly or by a cougar, that the mother had returned and driven away the murderer, and that she had then buried the body and lain above it, waiting to wreak her vengeance on the first passer-by.

Old Tazewell Woody, during his thirty years' life as a hunter in the Rockies and on the great plains, killed very many grizzlies. He always exercised much caution in dealing with them; and, as it happened, he was by some suitable tree in almost every case when he was charged. He would accordingly climb the tree (a practice of which I do not approve however); and the bear would look up at him and pass on without stopping. Once, when he was hunting in the mountains with a companion, the latter, who was down in a valley, while Woody was on the hill-side, shot at a bear. The first thing Woody knew the wounded grizzly, running up-hill, was almost on him from behind. As he turned it seized his rifle in its jaws. He wrenched the rifle round, while the bear still gripped it, and pulled trigger, sending a bullet into its shoulder; whereupon it struck him with its paw, and knocked him over the rocks. By good luck he fell in a snow bank and was not hurt in the least. Meanwhile the bear went on and they never got it.

Once he had an experience with a bear which showed a very curious mixture of rashness and cowardice. He and a companion were camped in a little tepee or wigwam, with a bright fire in front of it, lighting up the night. There was an inch of snow on the ground. Just after they went to bed a grizzly came close to camp. Their dog rushed out and they could hear it bark round in the darkness for nearly an hour; then the bear drove it off and came right into camp. It went close to the fire, picking up the scraps of meat and bread, pulled a haunch of venison down from a tree, and passed and repassed in front of the tepee, paying no heed whatever to the two men, who crouched in the doorway talking to one another. Once it passed so close that Woody could almost have touched it. Finally his companion fired into it, and off it ran, badly wounded, without an attempt at retaliation. Next morning they followed its tracks in the snow, and found it a quarter of a mile away. It was near a pine and had buried itself under the loose earth, pine needles, and snow; Woody's companion almost walked over it, and putting his rifle to its ear blew out its brains.

In all his experience Woody had personally seen but four men who were badly mauled by bears. Three of these were merely wounded. One was bitten terribly in the back. Another had an arm partially chewed off. The third was a man named George Dow, and the accident happened to him on the Yellowstone, about the year 1878. He was with a pack animal at the time, leading it on a trail through a wood. Seeing a big she-bear with cubs he yelled at her; whereat she ran away, but only to cache her cubs, and in a minute, having hidden them, came racing back at him.

His pack animal being slow he started to climb a tree; but before he could get far enough up she caught him, almost biting a piece out of the calf of his leg, pulled him down, bit and cuffed him two or three times, and then went on her way.

The only time Woody ever saw a man killed by a bear was once when he had given a touch of variety to his life by shipping on a New Bedford whaler which had touched at one of the Puget Sound ports. The whaler went up to a part of Alaska where bears were very plentiful and bold. One day a couple of boats' crews landed; and the men, who were armed only with an occasional harpoon or lance, scattered over the beach, one of them, a Frenchman, wading into the water after shellfish. Suddenly a bear emerged from some bushes and charged among the astonished sailors, who scattered in every direction; but the bear, said Woody, "just had it in for that Frenchman," and went straight at him. Shrieking with terror he retreated up to his neck in the water; but the bear plunged in after him, caught him, and disemboweled him. One of the Yankee mates then fired a bomb lance into the bear's hips, and the savage beast hobbled off into the dense cover of the low scrub, where the enraged sailor folk were unable to get at it.

The truth is that while the grizzly generally avoids a battle if possible, and often acts with great cowardice, it is never safe to take liberties with him; he usually fights desperately and dies hard when wounded and cornered, and exceptional individuals take the aggressive on small provocation.

During the years I lived on the frontier I came in contact with many persons who had been severely mauled or even crippled for life by grizzlies; and a number of cases where they killed men outright were also brought under my ken. Generally these accidents, as was natural, occurred to hunters who had roused or wounded the game.

A fighting bear sometimes uses his claws and sometimes his teeth. I have never known one to attempt to kill an antagonist by hugging, in spite of the popular belief to this effect; though he will sometimes draw an enemy towards him with his paws the better to reach him with his teeth, and to hold him so that he cannot escape from the biting. Nor does the bear often advance on his hind legs to the attack; though, if the man has come close to him in thick underbrush, or has stumbled on him in his lair unawares, he will often rise up in this fashion and strike a single blow. He will also rise in clinching with a man on horseback. In 1882 a mounted Indian was killed in this manner on one of the river bottoms some miles below where my ranch house now stands, not far from the junction of the Beaver and Little Missouri. The bear had been hunted into a thicket by a band of Indians, in whose company my informant, a white squaw-man, with whom I afterward did some trading, was travelling. One of them in the excitement of the pursuit rode across the end of the thicket; as he did so the great beast sprang at him with wonderful quickness, rising on its hind legs, and knocking over the horse and rider with a single sweep of its terrible fore-paws. It then turned on the fallen man and tore him open, and though the other Indians came promptly to his rescue and slew his assailant, they were not in time to save their comrade's life.

A bear is apt to rely mainly on his teeth or claws according to whether his efforts are directed primarily to killing his foe or to making good his own escape. In the latter event he trusts chiefly to his claws. If cornered, he of course makes a rush for freedom, and in that case he downs any man who is in his way with a sweep of his great paw, but passes on without stopping to bite him. If while sleeping or resting in thick brush someone suddenly stumbles on him close up he pursues the same course, less from anger than from fear, being surprised and startled. Moreover, if attacked at close quarters by men and dogs he strikes right and left in defense.

Sometimes what is called a charge is rather an effort to get away. In localities where he has been hunted, a bear, like every other kind of game, is always on the look-out for an attack, and is prepared at any moment for immediate flight. He seems ever to have in his mind, whether feeding, sunning himself, or merely roaming around, the direction—usually towards the thickest cover or most broken ground—in which he intends to run if molested. When shot at he instantly starts towards this place; or he may be so confused that he simply runs he knows not whither; and in either event he may take a line that leads almost directly to or by the huter, although he had at first no thought of charging. In such a case he usually strikes a single knock-down blow and gallops on without halting, though that one blow may have taken life. If the claws are long and fairly sharp (as in early spring, or even in the fall, if the animal has been working over soft ground) they add immensely to the effect of the blow, for they cut like blunt axes. Often, however, late in the season, and if the ground has been dry and hard, or rocky, the claws are worn down nearly to the quick, and the blow is then given mainly with the under side of the paw; although even under this disadvantage a thump from a big bear will down a horse or smash in a man's breast. The hunter Hofer once lost a horse in this manner. He shot at and wounded a bear which rushed off, as ill luck would have it, past the place where his horse was picketed; probably more in fright than in anger it struck the poor beast a blow which, in the end, proved mortal.

If a bear means mischief and charges not to escape but to do damage, its aim is to grapple with or throw down its foe and bite him to death. The charge is made at a gallop, the animal sometimes coming on silently, with the mouth shut, and sometimes with the jaws open, the lips drawn back and teeth showing, uttering at the same time a succession of roars or of savage rasping snarls. Certain bears charge without any bluster and perfectly straight; while others first threaten and bully, and even when charging stop to growl, shake the head, and bite at a bush or knock holes in the ground with their fore-paws. Again, some of them charge home with a ferocious resolution which their extreme tenacity of life renders especially dangerous; while others can be turned or driven back even by a shot which is not mortal. They show the same variability in their behavior when wounded. Often a big bear, especially if charging, will receive a bullet in perfect silence, without flinching or seeming to pay any heed to it; while another will cry out and tumble about, and if charging, even though it may not abandon the attack, will pause for a moment to whine or bite at the wound.

Sometimes a single bite causes death. One of the most successful bear hunters I ever knew, an old fellow whose real name I never heard as he was always called Old Ike, was killed in this way in the spring or early summer of 1886 on one of the head-waters of the Salmon. He was a very good shot, had killed nearly a hundred bears with the rifle, and, although often charged, had never met with any accident, so that he had grown somewhat careless. On the day in question he had met a couple of mining prospectors and was travelling with them, when a grizzly crossed his path. The old hunter immediately ran after it, rapidly gaining, as the bear did not hurry when it saw itself pursued, but slouched slowly forwards, occasionally turning its head to grin and growl. It soon went into a dense grove of young spruce, and as the hunter reached the edge it charged fiercely out. He fired one hasty shot, evidently wounding the animal, but not seriously enough to stop or cripple it; and as his two companions ran forward they saw the bear seize him with its wide-spread jaws, forcing him to the ground. They shouted and fired, and the beast abandoned the fallen man on the instant and sullenly retreated into the spruce thicket, whither they dared not follow it. Their friend was at his last gasp; for the whole side of the chest had been crushed in by the one bite, the lungs showing between the rent ribs.

Very often, however, a bear does not kill a man by one bite, but after throwing him lies on him, biting him to death. Usually, if no assistance is at hand, such a man is doomed; although if he pretends to be dead, and has the nerve to lie quiet under very rough treatment, it is just possible that the bear may leave him alive, perhaps after half burying what it believes to be the body. In a very few exceptional instances men of extraordinary prowess with the knife have succeeded in beating off a bear, and even in mortally wounding it, but in most cases a single-handed struggle, at close quarters, with a grizzly bent on mischief, means death.

Occasionally the bear, although vicious, is also frightened, and passes on after giving one or two bites; and frequently a man who is knocked down is rescued by his friends before he is killed, the big beast mayhap using his weapons with clumsiness. So a bear may kill a foe with a single blow of its mighty fore-arm, either crushing in the head or chest by sheer force of sinew, or else tearing open the body with its formidable claws; and so on the other hand he may, and often does, merely disfigure or maim the foe by a hurried stroke. Hence it is common to see men who have escaped the clutches of a grizzly, but only at the cost of features marred beyond recognition, or a body rendered almost helpless for life. Almost every old resident of western Montana or northern Idaho has known two or three unfortunates who have suffered in this manner. I have myself met one such man in Helena, and another in Missoula; both were living at least as late as 1889, the date at which I last saw them. One had been partially scalped by a bear's teeth; the animal was very old and so the fangs did not enter the skull. The other had been bitten across the face, and the wounds never entirely healed, so that his disfigured visage was hideous to behold.

Most of these accidents occur in following a wounded or worried bear into thick cover; and under such circumstances an animal apparently hopelessly disabled, or in the death throes, may with a last effort kill one or more of its assailants. In 1874 my wife's uncle, Captain Alexander Moore, U.S.A., and my friend Captain Bates, with some men of the 2d and 3d Cavalry, were scouting in Wyoming, near the Freezeout Mountains. One morning they roused a bear in the open prairie and followed it at full speed as it ran towards a small creek. At one spot in the creek beavers had built a dam, and as usual in such places there was a thick growth of bushes and willow saplings. Just as the bear reached the edge of this little jungle it was struck by several balls, both of its fore-legs being broken. Nevertheless, it managed to shove itself forward on its hind-legs, and partly rolled, partly pushed itself into the thicket, the bushes though low being so dense that its body was at once completely hidden. The thicket was a mere patch of brush, not twenty yards across in any direction. The leading troopers reached the edge almost as the bear tumbled in. One of them, a tall and powerful man named Miller, instantly dismounted and prepared to force his way in among the dwarfed willows, which were but breast-high. Among the men who had ridden up were Moore and Bates, and also the two famous scouts, Buffalo Bill—long a companion of Captain Moore,—and California Joe, Custer's faithful follower. California Joe had spent almost all his life on the plains and in the mountains, as a hunter and Indian fighter; and when he saw the trooper about to rush into the thicket he called out to him not to do so, warning him of the danger. But the man was a very reckless fellow and he answered by jeering at the old hunter for his over-caution in being afraid of a crippled bear. California Joe made no further effort to dissuade him, remarking quietly: "Very well, sonny, go in; it's your own affair." Miller then leaped off the bank on which they stood and strode into the thicket, holding his rifle at the port. Hardly had he taken three steps when the bear rose in front of him, roaring with rage and pain. It was so close that the man had no chance to fire. Its fore-arms hung useless and as it reared unsteadily on its hind-legs, lunging forward at him, he seized it by the ears and strove to hold it back. His strength was very great, and he actually kept the huge head from his face and braced himself so that he was not overthrown; but the bear twisted its muzzle from side to side, biting and tearing the man's arms and shoulders. Another soldier jumping down slew the beast with a single bullet, and rescued his comrade; but though alive he was too badly hurt to recover and died after reaching the hospital. Buffalo Bill was given the bear-skin, and I believe has it now.

The instances in which hunters who have rashly followed grizzlies into thick cover have been killed or severely mauled might be multiplied indefinitely. I have myself known of eight cases in which men have met their deaths in this manner.

It occasionally happens that a cunning old grizzly will lie so close that the hunter almost steps on him; and he then rises suddenly with a loud, coughing growl and strikes down or seizes the man before the latter can fire off his rifle. More rarely a bear which is both vicious and crafty deliberately permits the hunter to approach fairly near to, or perhaps pass by, its hiding-place, and then suddenly charges him with such rapidity that he has barely time for the most hurried shot. The danger in such a case is of course great.

Ordinarily, however, even in the brush, the bear's object is to slink away, not to fight, and very many are killed even under the most unfavorable circumstances without accident. If an unwounded bear thinks itself unobserved it is not apt to attack; and in thick cover it is really astonishing to see how one of these large animals can hide, and how closely it will lie when there is danger. About twelve miles below my ranch there are some large river bottoms and creek bottoms covered with a matted mass of cottonwood, box-elders, bullberry bushes, rosebushes, ash, wild ,ums, and other bushes. These bottoms have harbored bears ever since I first saw them; but though, often in company with a large party, I have repeatedly beaten through them, and though we must at times have been very near indeed to the game, we never so much as heard it run.

When bears are shot, as they usually must be, in open timber or on the bare mountain, the risk is very much less. Hundreds may thus be killed with comparatively little danger; yet even under these circumstances they will often charge, and sometimes make their charge good. The spice of danger, especially to a man armed with a good repeating rifle, is only enough to add zest to the chase, and the chief triumph is in outwitting the wary quarry and getting within range. Ordinarily the only excitement is in the stalk, the bear doing nothing more than keep a keen look-out and manifest the utmost anxiety to get away. As is but natural, accidents occasionally occur; yet they are usually due more to some failure in man or weapon than to the prowess of the bear. A good hunter whom I once knew, at a time when he was living in Butte, received fatal injuries from a bear he attacked in open woodland. The beast charged after the first shot, but slackened its pace on coming almost up to the man. The latter's gun jammed, and as he was endeavoring to work it he kept stepping slowly back, facing the bear which followed a few yards distant, snarling and threatening. Unfortunately while thus walking backwards the man struck a dead log and fell over it, whereupon the beast instantly sprang on him and mortally wounded him before help arrived.

On rare occasions men who are not at the time hunting it fall victims to the grizzly. This is usually because they stumble on it unawares and the animal attacks them more in fear than in anger. One such case, resulting fatally, occurred near my own ranch. The man walked almost over a bear while crossing a little point of brush, in a bend of the river, and was brained with a single blow of the paw. In another instance which came to my knowledge the man escaped with a shaking up, and without even a fright. His name was Perkins, and he was out gathering huckleberries in the woods on a mountain side near Pend'Oreille Lake. Suddenly he was sent flying head over heels, by a blow which completely knocked the breath out of his body; and so instantaneous was the whole affair that all he could ever recollect about it was getting a vague glimpse of the bear just as he was bowled over. When he came to he found himself lying some distance down the hill-side, much shaken, and without his berry pail, which had rolled a hundred yards below him, but not otherwise the worse for his misadventure; while the footprints showed that the bear, after delivering the single hurried stroke at the unwitting disturber of its daydreams, had run off uphill as fast as it was able.

A she-bear with cubs is a proverbially dangerous beast; yet even under such conditions different grizzlies act in directly opposite ways. Some she-grizzlies, when their cubs are young, but are able to follow them about, seem always worked up to the highest pitch of anxious and jealous rage, so that they are likely to attack unprovoked any intruder or even passer-by. Others when threatened by the hunter leave their cubs to their fate without a visible qualm of any kind, and seem to think only of their own safety.

In 1882 Mr. Caspar W. Whitney, now of New York, met with a very singular adventure with a she-bear and cub. He was in Harvard when I was, but left it and, like a good many other Harvard men of that time, took to cow-punching in the West. He went on a ranch in Rio Arriba County, New Mexico, and was a keen hunter, especially fond of the chase of cougar, bear, and elk. One day while riding a stony mountain trail he saw a little grizzly cub watching him from the chaparral above, and he dismounted to try to capture it; his rifle was a 40-90 Sharp's. Just as he neared the cub, he heard a growl and caught a glimpse of the old she, and he at once turned uphill, and stood under some tall, quaking aspens. From this spot he fired at and wounded the she, then seventy yards off; and she charged furiously. He hit her again, but as she kept coming like a thunderbolt he climbed hastily up the aspen, dragging his gun with him, as it had a strap. When the bear reached the foot of the aspen she reared, and bit and clawed the slender trunk, shaking it for a moment, and he shot her through the eye. Off she sprang for a few yards, and then spun round a dozen times, as if dazed or partially stunned; for the bullet had not touched the brain. Then the vindictive and resolute beast came back to the tree and again reared up against it; this time to receive a bullet that dropped her lifeless. Mr. Whitney then climbed down and walked to where the cub had been sitting as a looker-on. The little animal did not move until he reached out his hand; when it suddenly struck at him like an angry cat, dove into the bushes, and was seen no more.

In the summer of 1888 an old-time trapper, named Charley Norton, while on Loon Creek, of the middle fork of the Salmon, meddled with a she and her cubs. She ran at him and with one blow of her paw almost knocked off his lower jaw; yet he recovered, and was alive when I last heard of him.

Yet the very next spring the cowboys with my own wagon on the

Little Missouri round-up killed a mother bear which made but little more fight than a coyote. She had two cubs, and was surprised in the early morning on the prairie far from cover. There were eight or ten cowboys together at the time, just starting off on a long circle, and of course they all got down their ropes in a second, and putting spurs to their fiery little horses started toward the bears at a run, shouting and swinging their loops round their heads. For a moment the old she tried to bluster and made a half-hearted threat of charging; but her courage failed before the rapid onslaught of her yelling, rope-swinging assailants; and she took to her heels and galloped off, leaving the cubs to shift for themselves. The cowboys were close behind, however, and after half a mile's run she bolted into a shallow cave or hole in the side of a butte, where she stayed cowering and growling, until one of the men leaped off his horse, ran up to the edge of the hole, and killed her with a single bullet from his revolver, fired so close that the powder burned her hair. The unfortunate cubs were roped, and then so dragged about that they were speedily killed instead of being brought alive to camp, as ought to have been done.

In the cases mentioned above the grizzly attacked only after having been itself assailed, or because it feared an assault, for itself or for its young. In the old days, however, it may almost be said that a grizzly was more apt to attack than to flee. Lewis and Clark and the early explorers who immediately succeeded them, as well as the first hunters and trappers, the "Rocky Mountain men" of the early decades of the present [nineteenth] century, were repeatedly assailed in this manner; and not a few of the bear hunters of that period found that it was unnecessary to take much trouble about approaching their quarry, as the grizzly was usually prompt to accept the challenge and to advance of its own accord, as soon as it discovered the foe. All this is changed now. Yet even at the present day an occasional vicious old bear may be found, in some far off and little trod fastness, which still keeps up the former habit of its kind. All old hunters have tales of this sort to relate, the prowess, cunning, strength, and ferocity of the grizzly being favorite topics for camp-fire talk throughout the Rockies; but in most cases it is not safe to accept these stories without careful sifting.

Still, it is just as unsafe to reject them all. One of my own cowboys was once attacked by a grizzly, seemingly in pure wantonness. He was riding up a creek bottom, and had just passed a clump of rose and bullberry bushes when his horse gave such a leap as almost to unseat him, and then darted madly forward. Turning round in the saddle to his utter astonishment he saw a large bear galloping after him, at the horse's heels. For a few jumps the race was close, then the horse drew away and the bear wheeled and went into a thicket of wild plums. The amazed and indignant cowboy, as soon as he could rein in his steed, drew his revolver and rode back to and around the thicket, endeavoring to provoke his late pursuer to come out and try conclusions on more equal terms; but prudent Ephraim had apparently repented of his freak of ferocious bravado, and declined to leave the secure shelter of the jungle.

Other attacks are of a much more explicable nature. Mr. Huffman, the photographer, of Miles City, informed me that once when butchering some slaughtered elk he was charged twice by a she-bear and two well-grown cubs. This was a piece of sheer bullying, undertaken solely with the purpose of driving away the man and feasting on the carcasses; for in each charge the three bears, after advancing with much blustering, roaring, and growling, halted just before coming to close quarters. In another instance a gentleman I once knew, a Mr. S. Carr, was charged by a grizzly from mere ill temper at being disturbed at meal-time. The man was riding up a valley; and the bear was at an elk carcass, near a clump of firs. As soon as it became aware of the approach of the horseman, while he was yet over a hundred yards distant, it jumped on the carcass, looked at him a moment, and then ran straight for him. There was no particular reason why it should have charged, for it was fat and in good trim, though when killed its head showed scars made by the teeth of rival grizzlies. Apparently it had been living so well, principally on flesh, that it had become quarrelsome; and perhaps its not over sweet disposition had been soured by combats with others of its own kind. In yet another case, a grizzly charged with even less excuse. An old trapper, from whom I occasionally bought fur, was toiling up a mountain pass when he spied a big bear sitting on his haunches on the hill-side above. The trapper shouted and waved his cap; whereupon, to his amazement, the bear uttered a loud "wough" and charged straight down on him—only to fall a victim to misplaced boldness.

I am even inclined to think that there have been wholly exceptional occasions when a grizzly has attacked a man with the deliberate purpose of making a meal of him; when, in other words, it has started on the career of a man-eater. At least, on any other theory I find it difficult to account for an attack which once came to my knowledge. I was at Sand Point, on Pend'Oreille Lake, and met some French and Méti trappers, then in town with their bales of beaver, otter, and sable. One of them, who gave his name as Baptiste Lamoche, had his head twisted over to one side, the result of the bite of a bear. When the accident occurred he was out on a trapping trip with two companions. They had pitched camp right on the shore of a cove in a little lake, and his comrades were off fishing in a dugout or pirogue. He himself was sitting near the shore, by a little lean-to, watching some beaver meat which was sizzling over the dying embers. Suddenly, and without warning, a great bear, which had crept silently up beneath the shadows of the tall evergreens, rushed at him, with a guttural roar, and seized him before he could rise to his feet. It grasped him with its jaws at the junction of the neck and shoulder, making the teeth meet through bone, sinew, and muscle; and turning, racked off towards the forest, dragging with it the helpless and paralyzed victim. Luckily the two men in the canoe had just paddled round the point, in sight of, and close to, camp. The man in the bow, seeing the plight of his comrade, seized his rifle and fired at the bear. The bullet went through the beast's lungs, and it forthwith dropped its prey, and running off some two hundred yards, lay down on its side and died. The rescued man recovered full health and strength, but never again carried his head straight.

Old hunters and mountain-men tell many stories, not only of malicious grizzlies thus attacking men in camp, but also of their even dogging the footsteps of some solitary hunter and killing him when the favorable opportunity occurs. Most of these tales are mere fables; but it is possible that in altogether exceptional instances they rest on a foundation of fact. One old hunter whom I knew told me such a story. He was a truthful old fellow, and there was no doubt that he believed what he said, and that his companion was actually killed by a bear; but it is probable that he was mistaken in reading the signs of his comrade's fate, and that the latter was not dogged by the bear at all, but stumbled on him and was slain in the surprise of the moment.

At any rate, cases of wanton assaults by grizzlies are altogether out of the common. The ordinary hunter may live out his whole life in the wilderness and never know aught of a bear attacking a man unprovoked; and the great majority of bears are shot under circumstances of no special excitement, as they either make no fight at all, or, if they do fight, are killed before there is any risk of their doing damage. If surprised on the plains, at some distance from timber or from badly broken ground, it is no uncommon feat for a single horseman to kill them with a revolver. Twice of late years it has been performed in the neighborhood of my ranch. In both instances the men were not hunters out after game, but simply cowboys, riding over the range in early morning in pursuance of their ordinary duties among the cattle. I knew both men and have worked with them on the round-up. Like most cowboys they carried 44-calibre Colt revolvers, and were accustomed to and fairly expert in their use, and they were mounted on ordinary cow-ponies—quick, wiry, pluckly little beasts. In one case the bear was seen from quite a distance, lounging across a broad table-land. The cowboy, by taking advantage of a winding and rather shallow coulie, got quite close to him. He then scrambled out of the coulie, put spurs to his pony, and raced up to within fifty yards of the astonished bear ere the latter quite understood what it was that was running at him through the gray dawn. He made no attempt at fight, but ran at top speed towards a clump of brush not far off at the head of a creek. Before he could reach it, however, the galloping horse-man was alongside, and fired three shots into his broad back. He did not turn, but ran on into the bushes and then fell over and died.

In the other case the cowboy, a Texan, was mounted on a good cutting pony, a spirited, handy, agile little animal, but excitable, and with a habit of dancing, which rendered it difficult to shoot from its back. The man was with the round-up wagon, and had been sent off by himself to make a circle through some low, barren buttes, where it was not thought more than a few head of stock would be found. On rounding the corner of a small washout he almost ran over a bear which was feeding on the carcass of a steer that had died in an alkali hole. After a moment of stunned surprise the bear hurled himself at the intruder with furious impetuosity; while the cowboy, wheeling his horse on its haunches and dashing in the spurs, carried it just clear of his assailant's headlong rush. After a few springs he reined in and once more wheeled half round, having drawn his revolver, only to find the bear again charging and almost on him. This time he fired into it, near the joining of the neck and shoulder, the bullet going downwards into the chest hollow; and again by a quick dash to one side he just avoided the rush of the beast and the sweep of its mighty fore-paw. The bear then halted for a minute, and he rode close by it at a run, firing a couple of shots, which brought on another resolute charge. The ground was somewhat rugged and broken, but his pony was as quick on its feet as a cat, and never stumbled, even when going at full speed to avoid the bear's first mad rushes. It speedily became so excited, how-ever, as to render it almost impossible for the rider to take aim. Some-times he would come up close to the bear and wait for it to charge, which it would do, first at a trot, or rather rack, and then at a lumbering but swift gallop; and he would fire one or two shots before being forced to run. At other times, if the bear stood still in a good place, he would run by it, firing as he rode. He spent many cartridges, and though most of them were wasted, occasionally a bullet went home. The bear fought with the most savage courage, champing its bloody jaws, roaring with rage, and looking the very incarnation of evil fury. For some minutes it made no effort to flee, either charging or standing at bay. Then it began to move slowly towards a patch of ash and wild plums in the head of a coulie, some distance off. Its pursuer rode after it, and when close enough would push by it and fire, while the bear would spin quickly round and charge as fiercely as ever, though evidently beginning to grow weak. At last, when still a couple of hundred yards from cover the man found he had used up all his cartridges, and then merely followed at a safe distance. The bear no longer paid heed to him, but walked slowly forwards, swaying its great head from side to side, while the blood streamed from between its half-opened jaws. On reaching the cover he could tell by the waving of the bushes that it walked to the middle and then halted. A few minutes afterwards some of the other cowboys rode up, having been attracted by the incessant firing. They surrounded the thicket, firing and throwing stones into the bushes. Finally, as nothing moved, they ventured in and found the indomitable grizzly warrior lying dead.

Cowboys delight in nothing so much as the chance to show their skill as riders and ropers; and they always try to ride down and rope any wild animal they come across in favorable ground and close enough up. If a party of them meets a bear in the open they have great fun; and the struggle between the shouting, galloping rough-riders and their shaggy quarry is full of wild excitement and not unaccompanied by danger. The bear often throws the noose from his head so rapidly that it is a difficult matter to catch him; and his frequent charges scatter his tormentors in every direction while the horses become wild with fright over the roaring, bristling beast—for horses seem to dread a bear more than any other animal. If the bear cannot reach cover, however, his fate is sealed. Sooner or later, the noose tightens over one leg, or perchance over the neck and fore-paw, and as the rope straightens with a "pluck," the horse braces itself desperately and the bear tumbles over. Whether he regains his feet or not the cowboy keeps the rope taut; soon another noose tightens over a leg, and the bear is speedily rendered helpless.

I have known of these feats being performed several times in northern Wyoming, although never in the immediate neighborhood of my ranch. Mr. Archibald Roger's cowhands have in this manner caught several bears, on or near his ranch on the Gray Bull, which flows into the Bighorn; and those of Mr. G. B. Grinnell have also occasionally done so. Any set of moderately good ropers and riders, who are accustomed to back one another up and act together, can accomplish the feat if they have smooth ground and plenty of room. It is, however, indeed a feat of skill and daring for a single man; and yet I have known of more than one instance in which it has been accomplished by some reckless knight of the rope and the saddle. One such occurred in 1887 on the Flathead Reservation, the hero being a half-breed; and another in 1890 at the mouth of the Bighorn, where a cowboy roped, bound, and killed a large bear single-handed.

My friend General "Red" Jackson, of Bellemeade, in the pleasant mid-county of Tennessee, once did a feat which casts into the shade even the feats of the men of the lariat. General Jackson, who afterwards became one of the ablest and most renowned of the Confederate cavalry leaders, was at the time a young officer in the Mounted Rifle Regiment, now known as the 3d United States Cavalry. It was some years before the Civil War, and the regiment was on duty in the Southwest, then the debatable land of Comanche and Apache. While on a scout after hostile Indians, the troops in their march roused a large grizzly which sped off across the plain in front of them. Strict orders had been issued against firing at game, because of the nearness of the Indians. Young Jackson was a man of great strength, a keen swordsman, who always kept the finest edge on his blade, and he was on a swift and mettled Kentucky horse, which luckily had but one eye. Riding at full speed he soon overtook the quarry. As the horse hoofs sounded nearer, the grim bear ceased its flight, and whirling round stood at bay, raising itself on its hind-legs and threatening its pursuer with bared fangs and spread claws. Carefully riding his horse so that its blind side should be towards the monster, the cavalryman swept by at a run, handling his steed with such daring skill that he just cleared the blow of the dreaded fore-paw, while with one mighty sabre stroke he cleft the bear's skull, slaying the grinning beast as it stood upright.

"Buckskin and the Bear," from *The Youth's Companion*, July 13, 1893.

A
Man-Killing
Bear

Chapter VIII

Almost every trapper past middle age who has spent his life in the wilderness has stories to tell about exceptionally savage bears. One of these stories was told in my ranch house one winter evening by an old mountain hunter, clad in fur cap, buckskin hunting shirt and leather trousers, who had come to my ranch at nightfall, when the cowboys were returning from their day's labor.

The old fellow, who was known by the nickname of "Buckskin," had camped for several months in the Bad Lands but a score of miles away from my ranch. Most of his previous life had been spent among the main chains of the Rockies. After supper the conversation drifted to bears, always a favorite subject of talk in frontier cabins, and some of my men began to recount their own adventures with these great, clumsy-looking beasts.

This at once aroused the trapper's interest. He soon had the conversation to himself, telling us story after story of the bears he had killed and the escapes he had met with in battling against them.

In particular he told us of one bear which, many years before, had killed the partner with whom at the time he was trapping.

The two men were camped in a high mountain valley in northwestern Wyoming, their camp being pitched at the edge of a "park country"—that is, a region where large glades and groves of tall evergreen trees alternate.

They had been trapping beaver, the animal which, on account of its abundance and the value of the fur, was more eagerly followed than any other by the old-time plains and mountain trappers. They had with them four shaggy pack ponies, such as most of these hunters use, and as these ponies were not needed at the moment, they had been turned loose to shift for themselves in the open glade country.

Late one evening three of the ponies surprised the trappers by galloping up to the campfire and there halting. The fourth did not make his appearance. The trappers knew that some wild beast must have assailed the animals and had probably caught one and caused the others to flee toward the place which they had learned to associate with safety.

Before dawn the next morning the two men started off to look for the lost horse. They skirted several great glades, following the tracks of the ponies that had come to the fire the previous evening. Two miles away, at the edge of a tall pine wood, they found the body of the lost horse, already partially eaten.

The tracks round about showed that the assailant was a grizzly of uncommon size, which had evidently jumped at the horses just after dusk, as they fed up to the edge of the woods. The owner of the horse decided to wait by the carcass for the bear's return, while old Buckskin went off to do the day's work in looking after traps, and the like.

Buckskin was absent all day, and reached camp after nightfall. His friend had come in ahead of him, having waited in vain for the bear. As there was no moon he had not thought it worthwhile to stay by the bait during the night.

The next morning they returned to the carcass and found that the bear had returned and eaten his full, after which he had lumbered off up the hillside. They took up his tracks and followed him for some three hours; but the wary old brute was not to be surprised. When they at last reached the spot where he had made his bed, it was only to find that he must have heard them as they approached, for he had evidently left in a great hurry.

After following the roused animal for some distance they found they could not overtake him. He was in an ugly mood, and kept halting every mile or so to walk to and fro, bite and break down the saplings, and paw the earth and dead logs; but in spite of this bullying he would not absolutely await their approach, but always shambled off before they came in sight.

At last they decided to abandon the pursuit. They then separated, each to make an afternoon's hunt and return to camp by his own way.

Our friend reached camp at dusk, but his partner did not turn up that evening at all. However, it was nothing unusual for either one of the two to be off for a night, and Buckskin thought little of it.

Next morning he again hunted all day, and returned to camp fully expecting to see his friend there, but found no sign of him. The second night passed, still without his coming in.

The morning after, the old fellow became uneasy and started to hunt him up. All that day he searched in vain, and when, on coming back to camp, there was still no trace of him, he was sure that some accident had happened.

The next morning he went back to the pine grove in which they had separated on leaving the trail of the bear. His friend had worn hob-nail boots instead of moccasins, and this made it much easier to follow his tracks. With some difficulty the old hunter traced him for some four miles, until he came to a rocky stretch of country, where all sign of the footprints disappeared.

However, he was a little startled to observe footprints of a different sort. A great bear, without doubt the same one that had killed the horse, had been travelling in a course parallel to that of the man.

Apparently the beast had been lurking just in front of his two pursuers the day they followed him from the carcass; and from the character of the "sign" Buckskin judged that as soon as he separated from his friend, the bear had likewise turned and had begun to follow the trapper.

The bear had not followed the man into the rocky piece of ground, and when the old hunter failed in his efforts to trace up his friend, he took the trail of the bear instead.

Three-quarters of a mile on, the bear, which had so far been walking, broke into a gallop, the claws making deep scratches here and there in the patches of soft earth. The trail then led into a very thick and dark wood, and here the footprints of the man suddenly reappeared.

For some little time the old hunter was unable to make up his mind with certainty as to which one was following the other; but finally, in the decayed mold by a rotten log, he found unmistakable sign where the print of the bear's foot overlaid that of the man. This put the matter beyond doubt. The bear was following the man.

For a couple of hours more the hunter slowly and with difficulty followed the dim trail.

The bear had apparently not cared to close in, but had slouched along some distance behind the man. Then in a marshy thicket where a mountain stream came down, the end had come.

Evidently at this place the man, still unconscious that he was followed, had turned and gone upward, and the bear, altering his course to an oblique angle, had intercepted him, making his rush just as he came through a patch of low willows. The body of the man lay under the willow branches beside the brook, terribly torn and disfigured.

Evidently the bear had rushed at him so quickly that he could not fire his gun, and had killed him with its powerful jaws. The unfortunate man's body was almost torn to pieces. The killing had evidently been done purely for malice, for the remains were uneaten, nor had the bear returned to them.

Angry and horrified at his friend's fate, old Buckskin spent the next two days in looking carefully through the neighboring groves for fresh tracks of the cunning and savage monster. At last he found an open spot of ground where the brute was evidently fond of sunning himself in the early morning, and to this spot the hunter returned before dawn the following day.

He did not have long to wait. By sunrise a slight crackling of the thick undergrowth told him that the bear was approaching. A few minutes afterward the brute appeared. It was a large beast with a poor coat, its head scarred by teeth and claw marks gained in many a combat with others of its own kind.

It came boldly into the opening and lay down, but for some time kept turning its head from side to side so that no shot could be obtained.

At last, growing impatient, the hunter broke a stick. Instantly the bear swung his head around sidewise, and in another moment a bullet crashed into its skull at the base of the ear, and the huge body fell limply over on its side, lifeless.

"Pack train coming out of the Mountains," from *Hunting Trips of a Ranchman.*

A
Mysterious
Enemy
Chapter IX

Frontiersmen are not, as a rule, apt to be very superstitious. They lead lives too hard and practical, and have too little imagination in things spiritual and supernatural. I have heard but few ghost stories while living on the frontier, and these few were of a perfectly commonplace and conventional type.

But I once listened to a goblin story which rather impressed me. It was told by a grisled, weather-beaten old mountain hunter, named Bauman, who was born and had passed all his life on the frontier. He must have believed what he said, for he could hardly repress a shudder at certain points of the tale; but he was of German ancestry, and in childhood had doubtless been saturated with all kinds of ghost and goblin lore, so that many fearsome superstitions were latent in his mind; besides, he knew well the stories told by the Indian medicine men in their winter camps, of the snow-walkers, and the spectres, and the formless evil beings that haunt the forest depths, and dog and waylay the lonely wanderer who after nightfall passes through the regions where they lurk; and it may be that when overcome by the horror of the fate that befell his friend, and when oppressed by the awful dread of the unknown, he grew to attribute, both at the time and still more in remembrance, weird and elfin traits to what was merely some abnormally wicked and cunning wild beast; but whether this was so or not, no man can say.

When the event occurred Bauman was still a young man, and was trapping with a partner among the mountains dividing the forks of the Salmon from the head of Wisdom River. Not having had much luck, he and his partner determined to go up into a particularly wild and lonely pass through which ran a small stream said to contain many beaver. The pass had an evil reputation because the year before a solitary hunter who had wandered into it was there slain, seemingly by a wild beast, the half-eaten remains being afterwards found by some mining prospectors who had passed his camp only the night before.

The memory of this event, however, weighed very lightly with the two trappers, who were as adventurous and hardy as others of their kind. They took their two lean mountain ponies to the foot of the pass, where they left them in an open beaver meadow, the rocky timber-clad ground being from thence onwards impracticable for horses. They then struck out on foot through the vast, gloomy forest, and in about four hours reached a little open glade where they concluded to camp, as signs of game were plenty.

There was still an hour or two of daylight left, and after building a brush lean-to and throwing down and opening their packs, they started up stream. The country was very dense and hard to travel through, as there was much down timber, although here and there the sombre woodland was broken by small glades of mountain grass.

At dusk they again reached camp. The glade in which it was pitched was not many yards wide, the tall, close-set pines and firs rising round it like a wall. On one side was a little stream, beyond which rose the steep mountain-slopes, covered with the unbroken growth of the evergreen forest.

They were surprised to find that during their short absence something, apparently a bear, had visited camp, and had rummaged about among their things, scattering the contents of their packs, and in sheer wantonness destroying their lean-to. The footprints of the beast were quite plain, but at first they paid no particular heed to them, busying themselves with rebuilding the lean-to, laying out their beds and stores, and lighting the fire.

While Bauman was making ready supper, it being already dark, his companion began to examine the tracks more closely, and soon took a brand from the fire to follow them up, where the intruder had walked along a game trail after leaving the camp. When the brand flickered out, he returned and took another, repeating his inspection of the footprints very closely. Coming back to the fire, he stood by it a minute or two, peering out into the darkness, and suddenly remarked: "Bauman, that bear has been walking on two legs." Bauman laughed at this, but his partner insisted that he was right, and upon again examining the tracks with a torch, they certainly did seem to be made by but two paws, or feet. However, it was too dark to make sure. After discussing whether the footprints could possibly be those of a human being, and coming to the conclusion that they could not be, the two men rolled up in their blankets, and went to sleep under the lean-to.

At midnight Bauman was awakened by some noise, and sat up in his blankets. As he did so his nostrils were struck by a strong, wild-beast odor, and he caught the loom of a great body in the darkness at the mouth of the lean-to. Grasping his rifle, he fired at the vague, threatening shadow, but must have missed, for immediately afterwards he heard the smashing of the underwood as the thing, whatever it was, rushed off into the impenetrable blackness of the forest and the night.

After this the two men slept but little, sitting up by the rekindled fire, but they heard nothing more. In the morning they started out to look at the few traps they had set the previous evening and to put out new ones. By an unspoken agreement they kept together all day, and returned to camp towards evening.

On nearing it they saw, hardly to their astonishment, that the lean-to had been again torn down. The visitor of the preceding day had returned, and in wanton malice had tossed about their camp kit and bedding, and destroyed the shanty. The ground was marked up by its tracks, and on leaving the camp it had gone along the soft earth by the brook, where the footprints were as plain as if on snow, and, after a careful scrutiny of the trail, it certainly did seem as if, whatever the thing was, it had walked off on but two legs.

The men, thoroughly uneasy, gathered a great heap of dead logs, and kept up a roaring fire throughout the night, one or the other sitting on guard most of the time. About midnight the thing came down through the forest opposite, across the brook, and stayed there on the hill-side for nearly an hour. They could hear the branches crackle as it moved about, and several times it uttered a harsh, grating, long-drawn moan, a peculiarly sinister sound. Yet it did not venture near the fire.

In the morning the two trappers, after discussing the strange events of the last thirty-six hours, decided that they would shoulder their packs and leave the valley that afternoon. They were the more ready to do this because in spite of seeing a good deal of game sign they had caught very little fur. However, it was necessary first to go along the line of their traps and gather them, and this they started out to do.

All the morning they kept together, picking up trap after trap, each one empty. On first leaving camp they had the disagreeable sensation of being followed. In the dense spruce thickets they occasionally heard a branch snap after they had passed; and now and then there were slight rustling noises among the small pines to one side of them.

At noon they were back within a couple of miles of camp. In the high, bright sunlight their fears seemed absurd to the two armed men, accustomed as they were, through long years of lonely wandering in the wilderness to face every kind of danger from man, brute, or element. There were still three beaver traps to collect from a little pond in a wide ravine near by. Bauman volunteered to gather these and bring them in, while his companion went ahead to camp and make ready the packs.

On reaching the pond Bauman found three beaver in the traps, one of which had been pulled loose and carried into a beaver house. He took several hours in securing and preparing the beaver, and when he started homewards he marked with some uneasiness how low the sun was getting. As he hurried towards camp, under the tall trees, the silence and desolation of the forest weighed on him. His feet made no sound on the pine needles, and the slanting sun rays, striking through among the straight trunks, made a gray twilight in which objects at a distance glimmered indistinctly. There was nothing to break the ghostly stillness which, when there is no breeze, always broods over these sombre primeval forests.

At last he came to the edge of the little glade where the camp lay, and shouted as he approached it, but got no answer. The camp fire had gone out, though the thin blue smoke was still curling upwards. Near it lay the packs, wrapped and arranged. At first Bauman could see nobody; nor did he receive an answer to his call. Stepping forward he again shouted, and as he did so his eye fell on the body of his friend, stretched beside the trunk of a great fallen spruce. Rushing towards it the horrified trapper found that the body was still warm, but that the neck was broken, while there were four great fang marks in the throat.

The footprints of the unknown beast-creature, printed deep in the soft soil, told the whole story.

The unfortunate man, having finished his packing, had sat down on the spruce log with his face to the fire, and his back to the dense woods, to wait for his companion. While thus waiting, his monstrous assailant, which must have been lurking nearby in the woods, waiting for a chance to catch one of the adventurers unprepared, came silently up from behind, walking with long, noiseless steps, and seemingly still on two legs. Evidently unheard, it reached the man, and broke his neck by wrenching his head back with its forepaws, while it buried its teeth in his throat. It had not eaten the body, but apparently had romped and gambolled round it in uncouth, ferocious glee, occasionally rolling over and over it; and had then fled back into the soundless depths of the woods.

Bauman, utterly unnerved, and believing that the creature with which he had to deal was something either half human or half devil, some great goblin-beast, abandoned everything but his rifle and struck off at speed down the pass, not halting until he reached the beaver meadows where the hobbled ponies were still grazing. Mounting, he rode onwards through the night, until far beyond the reach of pursuit.

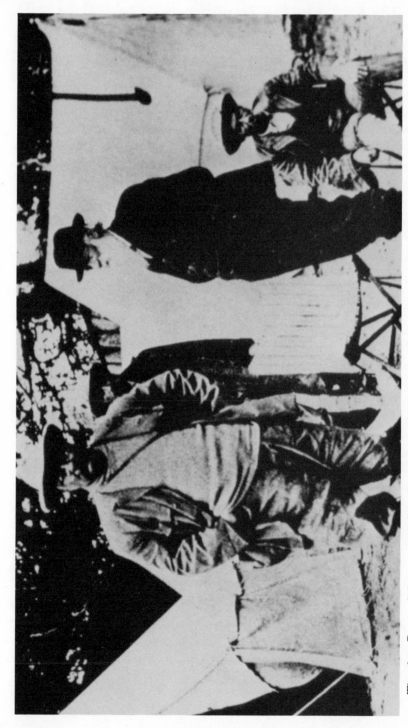

Theodore Roosevelt in camp with John Burroughs in Yellowstone in 1902.   Courtesy of the American Museum of Natural History.

Bears
in the
Yellowstone
Chapter X

It was in the interior of the Park, at the hotels beside the lake, the falls, and the various geyser basins, that we would have seen the bears had the season been late enough; but unfortunately the bears were still for the most part hibernating. We saw two or three tracks, but the animals themselves had not yet begun to come about the hotels. Nor were the hotels open. No visitors had previously entered the Park in the winter or early spring, the scouts and other employees being the only ones who occasionally traverse it. I was sorry not to see the bears, for the effect of protection upon bear life in the Yellowstone has been one of the phenomena of natural history. Not only have they grown to realize that they are safe, but, being natural scavengers and foul feeders, they have come to recognize the garbage heaps of the hotels as their special sources of food supply. Throughout the summer months they come to all the hotels in numbers, usually appearing in the late afternoon or evening, and they have become as indifferent to the presence of men as the deer themselves—some of them very much more indifferent. They have now taken their place among the recognized sights of the Park, and the tourists are nearly as much interested in them as in the geysers. In mussing over the garbage heaps they sometimes get tin cans stuck on their paws, and the result is painful. Buffalo Jones and some of the other scouts in extreme cases rope the bear, tie him up, cut the tin can off his paw, and let him go again. It is not an easy feat, but the astonishing thing is that it should be performed at all.

TEDDY BIDS THEM ALL GOOD-BYE THIS MORNING.

Cartoon spoofing Roosevelt's Yellowstone visit of 1902, from the Anaconda (Montana) *Standard*, April 24, 1902.

It was amusing to read the proclamations addressed to the tourists by the Park management, in which they were solemnly warned that the bears were really wild animals, and that they must on no account be either fed or teased. It is curious to think that the descendants of the great grizzlies which were the dread of the early explorers and hunters should now be semi-domesticated creatures, boldly hanging around crowded hotels for the sake of what they can pick up, and quite harmless so long as any reasonable precaution is exercised. They are much safer, for instance, than any ordinary bull or stallion, or even ram, and, in fact, there is no danger from them at all unless they are encouraged to grow too familiar or are in some way molested. Of course among the thousands of tourists there is a percentage of fools; and when fools go out in the afternoon to look at the bears feeding they occasionally bring themselves into jeopardy by some senseless act. The black bears and the cubs of the bigger bears can readily be driven up trees, and some of the tourists occasionally do this. Most of the animals never think of resenting it; but now and then one is run across which has its feelings ruffled by the performance. In the summer of 1902 the result proved disastrous to a too inquisitive tourist. He was travelling with his wife, and at one of the hotels they went out toward the garbage pile to see the bears feeding. The only bear in sight was a large she, which, as it turned out, was in a bad temper because another party of tourists a few minutes before had been chasing her cubs up a tree. The man left his wife and walked toward the bear to see how close he could get. When he was some distance off she charged him, whereupon he bolted back toward his wife. The bear overtook him, knocked him down and bit him severely. But the man's wife, without hesitation, attacked the bear with that thoroughly feminine weapon, an umbrella, and frightened her off. The man spent several weeks in the Park hospital before he recovered. Perhaps the following telegram sent by the manager of the Lake Hotel to Major Pitcher illustrates with sufficient clearness the mutual relations of the bears, the tourists, and the guardians of the public weal in the Park. The original was sent me by Major Pitcher. It runs:

"Lake. 7-27-'03. Major Pitcher, Yellowstone: As many as seventeen bears in an evening appear on my garbage dump. To-night eight or ten. Campers and people not of my hotel throw things at them to make them run away. I cannot, unless there personaly, control this. Do you think you could detail a trooper to be there every evening from say six o'clock until dark and make people remain behind danger line laid out by Warden Jones? Otherwise I fear some accident. The arrest of one or two of these campers might help. My own guests do pretty well as they are told. James Barton Key. 9 A.M."

Major Pitcher issued the order as requested.

At times the bears get so bold that they take to making inroads on the kitchen. One completely terrorized a Chinese cook. It would drive him off and then feast upon whatever was left behind. When a bear begins to act in this way or to show surliness it is sometimes necessary to shoot it. Other bears are tamed until they will feed out of the hand, and will come at once if called. Not only have some of the soldiers and scouts tamed bears in this fashion, but occasionally a chambermaid or waiter girl at one of the hotels has thus developed a bear as a pet.

This whole episode of bear life in the Yellowstone is to extraordinary that it will be well worth while for any man who has the right powers and enough time, to make a complete study of the life and history of the Yellowstone bears. Indeed, nothing better could be done by some of our out-door faunal naturalists than to spend at least a year in the Yellowstone, and to study the life habits of all the wild creatures therein. A man able to do this, and to write down accurately and interestingly what he has seen, would make a contribution of permanent value to our nature literature.

Roosevelt with the largest bear that he killed in Colorado. Courtesy of the
Theodore Roosevelt Collection, Harvard College Library.

A Colorado Bear Hunt

Chapter XI

In mid-April, nineteen hundred and five, our party, consisting of Philip B. Stewart, of Colorado Springs, and Dr. Alexander Lambert, of New York, in addition to myself, left Newcastle, Col., for a bear hunt. As guides and hunters we had John Goff and Jake Borah, than whom there are no better men at their work of hunting bear in the mountains with hounds. Each brought his own dogs; all told, there were twenty-six hounds, and four half-blood terriers to help worry the bear when at bay. We travelled in comfort, with a big pack train, spare horses for each of us, and a cook, packers, and horse wranglers. I carried one of the new model Springfield military rifles, a 30-40, with a soft-nosed bullet – a very accurate and hard-hitting gun.

    This first day we rode about twenty miles to where camp was pitched on the upper waters of East Divide Creek. It was a picturesque spot. At this altitude it was still late winter and the snow lay in drifts, even in the creek bottom, while the stream itself was not yet clear from ice. The tents were pitched in a grove of leafless aspens and great spruces, beside the rushing, ice-rimmed brook. The cook tent, with its stove, was an attractive place on the cool mornings and in stormy weather. Fry, the cook, a most competent man, had rigged up a table, and we had folding camp-chairs – luxuries utterly unknown to my former camping trips. Each day we breakfasted early and dined ten or twelve hours later, on returning from the day's hunt; and as we carried no lunch, the two meals were enjoyed with ravenous pleasure by the entire company. The horses were stout, tough, shaggy beasts, of wonderful staying power, and able to climb like cats. The country was very steep and rugged; the mountain-sides were greasy and slippery from the melting snow, while the snow bucking through the deep drifts on their tops and on the north sides was exhausting. Only sure-footed animals could avoid serious tumbles, and only animals of great endurance could have lasted through the work. Both Johnny Goff and his partner, Brick Wells, who often accompanied us on the hunts, were frequently mounted on animals of uncertain temper, with a tendency to buck on insufficient provocation; but they rode them with entire indifference up and down any incline. One of the riders, "Al," a very good tempered man, a tireless worker, had as one of his horses a queer, bigheaded dun beast, with a black stripe down its back and traces of zebra-like bands on the backs of his front legs. He was an atavistic animal, looking much as the horses must have looked which an age or two ago lived in this very locality and were preyed on by sabre-toothed tigers, hyenadons, and other strange and terrible beasts of a long-vanished era. Lambert remarked to him: "Al, you ought to call that horse of yours 'Fossil'; he is a hundred thousand years old." To which Al, with immovable face, replied: "Gee! and that man sold him to me for a seven-year-old! I'll have the law on him!"

The hounds were most interesting, and showed all the variations of character and temper to be expected in such a pack; a pack in which performance counted for everything and pedigree for nothing. One of the best hounds was half fox terrier. Three of Johnny's had been with us four years before, when he and I hunted cougars together; these three being Jim, now an old dog, who dropped behind in a hard run, but still excellent on a cold trail; Tree'em, who, like Jim, had grown aged, but was very sure; and Bruno, who had become one of the best of all the pack on a hot trail, but who was apt to overrun it if it became at all difficult and cold. The biggest dog of the pack, a very powerful animal, was Badge, who was half foxhound and half what Johnny called Siberian bloodhound—I suppose a Great Dane or Ulm dog. His full brother Bill came next to him. There was a Rowdy in Jake's pack and another Rowdy in Johnny's, and each got badly hurt before the hunt was through. Jake's Rowdy, as soon as an animal was killed, became very cross and wished to attack any dog that came near. One of Jake's best hounds was old Bruise, a very sure, although not a particularly fast dog. All the members of the pack held the usual wild-beast attitude toward one another. They joined together for the chase and the fight, but once the quarry was killed, their relations among themselves became those of active hostility or selfish indifference. At feeding time each took whatever his strength permitted, and each paid abject deference to whichever animal was his known superior in prowess. Some of the younger dogs would now and then run deer or coyote. But the older dogs paid heed only to bear and bobcat; and the pack, as a body, discriminated sharply between the hounds they could trust and those which would go off on a wrong trail. The four terriers included a heavy, liver-colored half-breed bull-dog, a preposterous animal who looked as if his ancestry had included a toadfish. He was a terrible fighter, but his unvarying attitude toward mankind was one of effusive and rather foolish affection. In a fight he could whip any of the hounds save Badge, and he was far more willing than Badge to accept punishment. There was also a funny little black and tan, named Skip, a most friendly little fellow, especially fond of riding in front or behind the saddle of any one of us who would take him up, although perfectly able to travel forty miles a day on his own sturdy legs if he had to, and then to join in the worry of the quarry when once it had been shot. Porcupines abounded in the woods, and one or two of the terriers and half a dozen of the hounds positively refused to learn any wisdom, invariably attacking each porcupine they found; the result being that we had to spend many minutes in removing the quills from their mouths, eyes, etc. A white bull-terrier would come in from such a combat with his nose literally looking like a glorified pincushion, and many of the spines we had to take out with nippers. The terriers never ran with the hounds, but stayed behind with the horses until they heard the hounds barking "bayed" or "treed," when they forthwith tore toward them. Skip adopted me as his special master, rode with me whenever I would let him, and slept on the foot of my bed at night, growling defiance at anything that came near. I grew attached to the friendly, bright little fellow, and at the end of the hunt took him home with me as a playmate for the children.

It was a great, wild country. In the creek bottoms there were a good many ranches; but we only occasionally passed by these, on our way to our hunting grounds in the wilderness along the edge of the snow-line. The mountains crowded close together in chain, peak, and tableland; all the higher ones were wrapped in an unrent shroud of snow. We saw a good many deer, and fresh sign of elk, but no elk themselves, although we were informed that bands were to be found in the high spruce timber where the snows were so deep that it would have been impossible to go on horseback, while going on foot would have been inconceivably fatiguing. The country was open. The high peaks were bare of trees. Cottonwoods, and occasionally dwarfed birch or

Setting out on the Colorado hunt. Courtesy of the Theodore Roosevelt Collection, Harvard College Library.

maple and willows, fringed the streams; aspens grew in groves higher up. There were pinyons and cedars on the slopes of the foothills; spruce clustered here and there in the cooler ravines and valleys and high up the mountains. The dense oak brush and thick growing cedars were hard on our clothes, and sometimes on our bodies.

Bear and cougars had once been very plentiful throughout this region, but during the last three or four years the cougars have greatly diminished in numbers throughout northern Colorado, and the bears have diminished also, although not to the same extent. The great grizzlies which were once fairly plentiful here are now very rare, as they are in most places in the United States. There remain plenty of the black and brown bears, which are simply individual color phases of the same species.

This Colorado trip was the first on which I hunted bears with hounds. If we had run across a grizzly there would doubtless have been a chance to show some prowess, at least in the way of hard riding. But the black and brown bears cannot, save under exceptional circumstances, escape from such a pack as we had with us; and the real merit of the chase was confined to the hounds and to Jake and Johnny for their skill in handling them. Perhaps I should add the horses, for their extraordinary endurance and surefootedness. As for the rest of us, we needed to do little more than to sit ten or twelve hours in the saddle and occasionally lead the horses up or down the most precipitous and cliff-like of the mountain sides. But it was great fun, nevertheless, and usually a chase lasted long enough to be interesting.

The first day after reaching camp we rode for eleven hours over a very difficult country, but without getting above the snow-line. Finally the dogs got on the fresh trail of a bobcat, and away they went. A bobcat will often give a good run, much better, on the average, than a cougar; and this one puzzled the dogs not a little at first. It scrambled out of one deep valley, crossing and recrossing the rock ledges where its scent was hard to follow; then plunged into another valley. Meanwhile we had ridden up on the high mountain spur between the two valleys, and after scrambling and galloping to and fro as the cry veered from point to point when the dogs changed directions, we saw them cross into the second valley. Here again they took a good deal of time to puzzle out the trail, and became somewhat scattered. We had dismounted and were standing by the horses' heads, listening to the baying and trying to decide which way we should go, when Stewart suddenly pointed us out a bear. It was on the other side of the valley from us, and perhaps half a mile away, galloping down hill, with two of the hounds after it, and in the sunlight its fur looked glossy black. In a minute or two it passed out of sight in the thick-growing timber at the bottom of the valley; and as we afterward found, the two hounds, getting momentarily thrown out, and hearing the others still baying on the cat trail, joined the latter. Jake started off to go around the head of the valley, while the rest of us plunged down into it. We found from the track that the bear had gone up the valley, and Jake found where he had come out on the high divide, and then turned and retraced his steps. But the hounds were evidently all after the cat. There was nothing for us to do but follow them. Sometimes riding, sometimes leading the horses, we went up the steep hillside, and as soon as we reached the crest heard the hounds barking treed. Shorty and Skip, who always trotted after the horses while the hounds were in full cry on a trail, recognized the change of note immediately, and tore off in the direction of the bay, while we followed as best we could, hoping to get there in time for Stewart and Lambert to take photographs of the lynx in a tree. But we were too late. Both Shorty and Skip could climb trees, and although Skip was too light to tackle a bobcat by himself, Shorty, a heavy, formidable dog, of unflinching courage and great physical strength, was altogether too much for any bobcat. When we reached the place we found the bobcat in the top of a pinyon, and Shorty steadily working his way up through the branches and very near the quarry. Evidently the bobcat felt that the situation needed the taking of desperate chances, and just before Shorty reached it out it jumped, Shorty yelling with excitement as he plunged down through the branches after it. But the cat did not jump far enough. One of the hounds seized it by the hind leg and in another second everything was over.

Shorty was always the first of the pack to attack dangerous game, and in attacking bear or cougar even Badge was much less reckless and more wary. In consequence, Shorty was seamed over with scars; most of them from bobcats, but one or two from cougars. He could speedily kill a bobcat single-handed; for these small lynxes are not really formidable fighters, although they will lacerate a dog quite severely. Shorty found a badger a much more difficult antagonist than a bobcat. A bobcat in a hole makes a hard fight, however. On this hunt we once got a bobcat under a big rock, and Jake's Rowdy in trying to reach it got so badly mauled that he had to join the invalid class for several days.

The bobcat we killed this first day was a male, weighing twenty-five pounds. It was too late to try after the bear, especially as we had only ten or a dozen dogs out, while the bear's tracks showed it to be a big one; and we rode back to camp.

A Colorado Bear Hunt

Next morning we rode off early, taking with us all twenty-six hounds and the four terriers. We wished first to find whether the bear had gone out of the country in which we had seen him, and so rode up a valley and then scrambled laboriously up the mountain-side to the top of the snow-covered divide. Here the snow was three feet deep in places, and the horses plunged and floundered as we worked our way in single file through the drifts. But it had frozen hard the previous night, so that a bear could walk on the crust and leave very little sign. In consequence we came near passing over the place where the animal we were after had actually crossed out of the canyon-like ravine in which we had seen him and gone over the divide into another set of valleys. The trail was so faint that it puzzled us, as we could not be certain how fresh it was, and until this point could be cleared up we tried to keep the hounds from following it. Old Jim, however, slipped off to one side and speedily satisfied himself that the trail was fresh. Along it he went, giving tongue, and the other dogs were maddened by the sound, while Jim, under such circumstances, paid no heed whatever to any effort to make him come back. Accordingly, the other hounds were slipped after him, and down they ran into the valley, while we slid, floundered, and scrambled along the ridge crest parallel to them, until a couple of miles farther on we worked our way down to some great slopes covered with dwarf scrub-oak. At the edge of these slopes, where they fell off in abrupt descent to the stream at the bottom of the valley, we halted. Opposite us was a high and very rugged mountain-side covered with a growth of pinyon—never a close-growing tree—its precipitous flanks broken by ledges and scored by gullies and ravines. It was hard to follow the scent across such a mountain-side, and the dogs speedily became much scattered. We could hear them plainly, and now and then could see them, looking like ants as they ran up and down hill and along the ledges. Finally we heard some of them barking bayed. The volume of sound increased steadily as the straggling dogs joined those which had first reached the hunted animal. At about this time, to our astonishment, Badge, usually a staunch fighter, rejoined us, followed by one or two other hounds, who seemed to have had enough of the matter. Immediately afterward we saw the bear, half-way up the opposite mountainside. The hounds were all around him, and occasionally bit at his hind quarters; but he had evidently no intention of climbing a tree. When we first saw him he was sitting up on a point of rock surrounded by the pack, his black fur showing to fine advantage. Then he moved off, threatening the dogs, and making what in Mississippi is called a walking bay. He was a sullen, powerful beast, and his leisurely gait showed how little he feared the pack, and how confident he was in his own burly strength. By this time the dogs had been after him for a couple of hours, and as there was no water on the mountain-side we feared they might be getting exhausted, and rode toward them as rapidly as we could. It was a hard climb up to where they were, and we had to lead the horses. Just as we came in sight of him, across a deep gully which ran down the sheer mountain-side, he broke bay and started off, threatening the foremost of the pack as they dared to approach him. They were all around him, and for a minute I could not fire; then as he passed under a pinyon I got a clear view of his great round stern and pulled trigger. The bullet broke both his hips, and he rolled down hill, the hounds yelling with excitement as they closed in on him. He could still play havoc with the pack, and there was need to kill him at once. I leaped and slid down on my side of the gully as he rolled down his; at the bottom he stopped and raised himself on his fore quarters; and with another bullet I broke his back between the shoulders.

Immediately all the dogs began to worry the carcass, while their savage baying echoed so loudly in the narrow, steep gully that we could with difficulty hear one another speak. It was a wild scene to look upon, as we scrambled down to where the dead bear lay on his back between the rocks. He did not die wholly unavenged, for he had killed one of the terriers and six other dogs were more or less injured. The chase of the bear is grim work for the pack. Jim, usually a very wary fighter, had a couple of deep holes in his thigh; but the most mishandled of the wounded dogs was Shorty. With his usual dauntless courage he had gone straight at the bear's head. Being such a heavy, powerful animal, I think if he had been backed up he could have held the bear's head down, and prevented the beast from doing much injury. As it was, the bear bit through the side of Shorty's head, and bit him in the shoulder, and again in the hip, inflicting very bad wounds. Once the fight was over Shorty lay down on the hillside, unable to move. When we started home we put him beside a little brook, and left a piece of bear meat by him, as it was obvious we could not get him to camp that day. Next day one of the boys went back with a pack-horse to take him in; but half-way out met him struggling toward camp, and returned. Late in the afternoon Shorty turned up while we were at dinner, and staggered toward us, wagging his tail with enthusiastic delight at seeing his friends. We fed him until he could not hold another mouthful; then he curled up in a dry corner of the cook-tent and slept for forty-eight hours; and two or three days afterward was able once more to go hunting.

The bear was a big male, weighing three hundred and thirty pounds. On examination at close quarters, his fur, which was in fine condition, was not as black as it had seemed when seen afar off, the roots of the hairs being brown. There was nothing whatever in his stomach. Evidently he had not yet begun to eat, and had been but a short while out of his hole. Bear feed very little when they first come out of their dens, sometimes beginning on grass, sometimes on buds. Occasionally they will feed at carcasses and try to kill animals within a week or two after they have left winter quarters, but this is rare, and as a usual thing for the first few weeks after they have come out they feed much as a deer would. Although not hog fat, as would probably have been the case in the fall, this bear was in good condition. In the fall, however, he would doubtless have weighed over four hundred pounds. The three old females we got on this trip weighed one hundred and eighty, one hundred and seventy-five, and one hundred and thirty-five pounds apiece. The yearlings weighed from thirty-one to forty pounds. The only other black bears I ever weighed all belonged to the sub-species *Luteolus*, and were killed on the Little Sunflower River, in Mississippi, in the late fall of nineteen hundred and two. A big old male, in poor condition, weighed two hundred and eighty-five pounds, and two very fat females weighed two hundred and twenty and two hundred and thirty-five pounds respectively.

The next few days we spent in hunting perseveringly, but unsuccessfully. Each day we were from six to twelve hours in the saddle, climbing with weary toil up the mountains and slipping and scrambling down them. On the tops and on the north slopes there was much snow, so that we had to pick our trails carefully, and even thus the horses often floundered belly-deep as we worked along in single file; the men on the horses which were best at snow bucking took turns in breaking the trail. In the worst places we had to dismount and lead the horses, often over such bad ground that nothing less sure-footed than the tough mountain ponies could even have kept their legs. The weather was cold, with occasional sharp flurries of snow, and once a regular snowstorm. We found the tracks of one or two bears, but in each case several days old, and it was evident either that the bears had gone back to their dens, finding the season so late, or else that they were lying quiet in sheltered places, and travelling as little as possible. One day, after a long run of certainly five or six miles through very difficult country, the dogs treed a bobcat in a big cedar. It had run so far that it was badly out of breath. Stewart climbed the tree and took several photographs of it, pushing the camera up to within about four feet of where the cat sat. Lambert obtained photographs of both Stewart and the cat. Shorty was at this time still an invalid from his encounter with the bear, but Skip worked his way thirty feet

The bear hunters at dinner, Colorado. Courtesy of the Theodore Roosevelt Collection, Harvard College Library.

up the tree in his effort to get at the bobcat. Lambert shot the latter with his revolver, the bobcat dying stuck in the branches; and he then had to climb the tree to get both the bobcat and Skip, as the latter was at such a height that we thought he would hurt himself if he fell. Another bobcat when treed sealed his own fate by stepping on a dead branch and falling right into the jaws of the pack.

At this camp, as everywhere, the tiny four-striped chipmunks were plentiful and tame; they are cheerful, attractive little animals. We also saw white-footed mice and a big meadow mouse around camp; and we found a young brushy-tailed pack-rat. The snowshoe rabbits were still white on the mountains, but in the lower valleys they had changed to the summer pelage. On the mountains we occasionally saw woodchucks and rock squirrels of two kinds, a large and a small—*Spermophilus grammurus* and *armatus*. The noisy, cheerful pine squirrels were common where the woods were thick. There were eagles and ravens in the mountains, and once we saw sandhill cranes soaring far above the highest peaks. The long-crested jays came familiarly around camp, but on this occasion we only saw the whiskey-jacks, Clark's nutcrackers and magpies, while off in the mountains. Among the pinyons, we several times came across strag-gling flocks of the queer pinyon jays or blue crows, with their unmistak-able calls and almost blackbird-like habits. There were hawks of several species, and blue grouse, while the smaller birds included flickers, robins, and the beautiful mountain bluebirds. Juncos and mountain chickadees were plentiful, and the ruby-crowned kinglets were singing with astonish-ing power for such tiny birds. We came on two nests of the red-tailed hawk; the birds were brooding, and seemed tame and unwary.

After a week of this we came to the conclusion that the snow was too deep and the weather too cold for us to expect to get any more bear in the immediate neighborhood, and accordingly shifted camp to where Clear Creek joins West Divide Creek.

The first day's hunt from the new camp was successful. We were absent about eleven hours and rode some forty miles. The day included four hours' steady snow bucking, for the bear, as soon as they got the chance, went through the thick timber where the snow lay deepest. Some two hours after leaving camp we found the old tracks of a she and a year-ling, but it took us a much longer time before we finally struck the fresh trail made late the previous night or early in the morning. It was Jake who first found this fresh track, while Johnny with the pack was a couple of miles away, slowly but surely puzzling out the cold trail and keeping the dogs up to their work. As soon as Johnny came up we put all the hounds on the tracks, and away they went, through and over the snow, yelling their eager delight. Meanwhile we had fixed our saddles and were ready for what lay ahead. It was wholly impossible to ride at the tail of the pack, but we did our best to keep within sound of the baying. Finally, after much hard work and much point riding through snow, slush, and deep mud, on the level, and along, up, and down sheer slopes, we heard the dogs barking treed in the middle of a great grove of aspens high up the mountainside. The snow was too deep for the horses, and leaving them, we trudged heavily up on foot. The yearling was in the top of a tall aspen. Lambert shot it with his rifle and we then put the dogs on the trail of the old she. Some of the young ones did not know what to make of this, evidently feeling that the tracks must be those of the bear that they had already killed; but the veterans were in fully cry at once. We scrambled after them up the steep mountain, and then downward along ridges and spurs, getting all the clear ground we could. Finally we had to take to the snow, and floundered and slid through the drifts until we were in the valley. Most of the time the dogs were within hearing, giving tongue as they followed the trail. Finally a total change in the note showed that they were barking treed; and as rapidly as possible we made our way toward the sound. Again we found ourselves unable to bring the horses up to where the bear had treed, and scrambled thither on foot through the deep snow.

The bear was some thirty or forty feet up a tall spruce; it was a big she, with a glossy black-brown coat. I was afraid that at our approach she might come down; but she had been running hard for some four hours, had been pressed close, and evidently had not the slightest idea of putting herself of her own free will within the reach of the pack, which was now frantically baying at the foot of the tree. I shot her through the heart. As the bullet struck she climbed up through the branches with great agility for six or eight feet; then her muscles relaxed, and down she came with a thud, nearly burying herself in the snow. Little Skip was one of the first dogs to seize her as she came down; and in another moment he literally disappeared under the hounds as they piled on the bear. As soon as possible we got off the skin and pushed campward at a good gait, for we were a long way off. Just at nightfall we came out on a bluff from which we could overlook the rushing, swirling brown torrent, on the farther bank of which the tents were pitched.

The stomach of this bear contained nothing but buds. Like the other shes killed on this trip, she was accompanied by her yearling young, but had no newly born cub; sometimes bear breed only every other year, but I have found the mother accompanied not only by her cub but by her young of the year before. The yearling also had nothing but buds in its stomach. When its skin was taken off, Stewart looked at it, shook his head, and turning to Lambert said solemnly, "Alex., that skin isn't big enough to use for anything but a doily." From that time until the end of the hunt the yearlings were only known as "doily bears."

Next morning we again went out, and this time for twelve hours steadily, in the saddle, and now and then on foot. Most of the time we were in snow, and it was extraordinary that the horses could get through it at all, especially in working up the steep mountain-sides. But until it got so deep that they actually floundered—that is, so long as they could get their legs down to the bottom—I found that they could travel much faster than I could. On this day some twenty good-natured, hard-riding young fellows from the ranches within a radius of a dozen miles had joined our party to "see the President kill a bear." They were a cheerful and eagerly friendly crowd, as hardy as so many young moose, and utterly fearless horsemen; one of them rode his wild, nervous horse bareback, because it had bucked so when he tried to put the saddle on it that morning that he feared he would get left behind, and so abandoned the saddle outright. Whenever they had a chance they all rode at headlong speed, paying no heed to the slope of the mountainside or the character of the ground. In the deep snow they did me a real service, for of course they had to ride their horses single file through the drifts, and by the time my turn came we had a good trail.

After a good deal of beating to and fro, we found where an old she-bear with two yearlings had crossed a hill during the night and put the hounds on their tracks. Johnny and Jake, with one or two of the cowboys, followed the hounds over the exceedingly difficult hillside where the trail led; or rather, they tried to follow them, for the hounds speedily got clear away, as there were many places where they could run on the crust of the snow, in which the horses wallowed almost helpless. The rest of us went down to the valley, where the snow was light and the going easier. The bear had travelled hither and thither through the woods on the sidehill, and the dogs became scattered. Moreover, they jumped several deer, and four or five of the young dogs took after one of the latter. Finally, however, the rest of the pack put up the three bears. We had an interesting glimpse of the chase as the bears quartered up across an open spot of the hillside. The hounds were but a short distance behind them, strung out in a long string, the more powerful, those which could do best in the snow-bucking, taking the lead. We pushed up the mountain-side after them, horse after horse getting down in the snow, and speedily heard the redoubled clamor which told us that something had been treed. It was half an hour before we could make our way to the tree, a spruce, in which the two yearlings had taken refuge, while around the bottom the entire pack was gathered, crazy with excitement. We could not take the yearlings alive, both because we lacked the means of carrying them, and because we were anxious to get after the old bear. We could not leave them where they were, because it would have been well-nigh impossible to get the dogs away, and because, even if we had succeeded in getting them away, they would not have run any other trail as long as they knew the yearlings were in the tree. It was therefore out of the question to leave them unharmed, as we should have been glad to do, and Lambert killed them both with his revolver; the one that was first hit immediately began biting its brother. The ranchmen took them home to eat.

The hounds were immediately put on the trail of the old one and disappeared over the snow. In a few minutes we followed. It was heavy work getting up the mountainside through the drifts, but once on top we made our way down a nearly bare spur, and then turned to the right, scrambled a couple of miles along a slippery sidehill, and halted. Below us lay a great valley, on the farther side of which a spruce forest stretched up toward the treeless peaks. Snow covered even the bottom of the valley, and lay deep and solid in the spruce forest on the mountain-side. The hounds were in full cry, evidently on a hot trail, and we caught glimpses of them far on the opposite side of the valley, crossing little open glades in the spruce timber. If the crust was hard they scattered out. Where it was at all soft they ran in single file. We worked our way down toward them, and on reaching the bottom of the valley, went up it as fast as the snow would allow. Finally we heard the pack again barking treed and started toward them. They had treed the bear far up the mountainside in the thick spruce timber, and a short experiment showed us that the horses could not possibly get through the snow. Accordingly, off we jumped and went toward the sound on foot, all the young ranchmen and cowboys rushing ahead, and thereby again making me an easy trail. On the way to the tree the rider of the bareback horse pounced on a snow-shoe rabbit which was crouched under a bush and caught it with his hands. It was half an hour before we reached the tree, a big spruce, up which the bear had gone to a height of some forty feet. I broke her neck with a single bullet. She was smaller than the one I had shot the day before, but full grown. In her stomach, as in those of the two yearlings, there were buds of rose-bushes and quaking aspens. One yearling had also swallowed a mouse. It was a long ride to camp, and darkness had fallen by the time we caught the gleam from the lighted tents, across the dark stream.

With neither of these last two bear had there been any call for prowess; my part was merely to kill the bear dead at the first shot, for the sake of the pack. But the days were very enjoyable, nevertheless. It was good fun to be twelve hours in the saddle in such wild and beautiful country, to look at and listen to the hounds as they worked, and finally to see the bear treed and looking down at the maddened pack baying beneath.

For the next two or three days I was kept in camp by a touch of Cuban fever. On one of these days Lambert enjoyed the longest hunt we had on the trip, after an old she-bear and three yearlings. The yearlings treed one by one, each of course necessitating a stoppage, and it was seven in the evening before the old bear at last went up a cottonwood and was shot; she was only wounded, however, and in the fight she crippled Johnny's Rowdy before she was killed. When the hunters reached camp it was thirteen hours since they had left it. The old bear was a very light brown; the first yearling was reddish-brown, the second light yellowish-brown, the third dark black-brown, though all were evidently of the same litter.

Following this came a spell of bad weather, snowstorm and blizzard steadily succeeding one another. This lasted until my holiday was over. Some days we had to stay in camp. On other days we hunted; but there was three feet of new snow on the summits and foothills, making it difficult to get about. We saw no more bear, and, indeed, no more beartracks that were less than two or three weeks old.

We killed a couple of bobcats. The chase of one was marked by several incidents. We had been riding through a blizzard on the top of a plateau, and were glad to plunge down into a steep sheer-sided valley. By the time we reached the bottom there was a lull in the storm and we worked our way with considerable difficulty through the snow, down timber, and lava rock, toward Divide Creek. After a while the valley widened a little, spruce and aspens fringing the stream at the bottom while the sides were bare. Here we struck a fresh bobcat trail leading off up one of the mountain-sides. The hounds followed it nearly to the top, then turned and came down again, worked through the timber in the bottom, and struck out on the hillside opposite. Suddenly we saw the bobcat running ahead of them and doubling and circling. A few minutes afterward the hounds followed the trail to the creek bottom and then began to bark treed. But on reaching the point we found there was no cat in the tree, although the dogs seemed certain that there was; and Johnny and Jake speedily had them again running on the trail. After making its way for some distance through the bottom, the cat had again taken to the sidehill, and the hounds went after it hard. Again they went nearly to the top, again they streamed down to the bottom and crossed the creek. Soon afterward we saw the cat ahead of them. For the moment it threw them off the track by making a circle and galloping around close to the rear-most hounds. It then made for the creek bottom, where it climbed to the top of a tall aspen. The hounds soon picked up the trail again, and followed it full cry; but unfortunately just before they reached where it had treed they ran on to a porcupine. When we reached the foot of the aspen, in the top of which the bobcat crouched, with most of the pack baying beneath, we found the porcupine dead and half a dozen dogs with their muzzles and throats filled full of quills. Before doing anything with the cat it was necessary to take these quills out. One of the terriers, which always found porcupines an irresistible attraction, was a really extra-ordinary sight, so thickly were the quills studded over his face and chest. But a big hound was in even worse condition; the quills were stuck in abundance into his nose, lips, cheeks, and tongue, and in the roof of his mouth they were almost as thick as bristles in a brush. Only by use of pincers was it possible to rid these two dogs of the quills, and it was a long and bloody job. The others had suffered less.

The dogs seemed to have no sympathy with one another, and apparently all that the rest of the pack felt was that they were kept a long time waiting for the cat. They never stopped baying for a minute, and Shorty, as was his habit, deliberately bit great patches of bark from the aspens, to show his impatience; for the tree in which the cat stood was not one which he could climb. After attending to the porcupine dogs one of the men climbed the tree and with a stick pushed out the cat. It dropped down through the branches forty or fifty feet, but was so quick in starting and dodging that it actually rushed through the pack, crossed the stream, and, doubling and twisting, was off up the creek through the timber. It ran cunning, and in a minute or two lay down under a bush and watched the hounds as they went by, overrunning its trail. Then it took off up the hillside; but the hounds speedily picked up its track, and running in single file, were almost on it. Then the cat turned down hill, but too late, for it was overtaken within fifty yards. This ended our hunting.

On Sunday we rode down some six miles from camp to a little blue school-house and attended service. The preacher was in the habit of riding over every alternate Sunday from Rifle, a little town twenty or twenty-five miles away; and the ranchmen with their wives and children, some on horseback, some in wagons, had gathered from thirty miles round to attend the service. The crowd was so large that the exercises had to take place in the open air, and it was pleasant to look at the strong frames and rugged, weather-beaten faces of the men; while as for the women, one respected them even more than the men.

In spite of the snowstorms spring was coming; some of the trees were beginning to bud and show green, more and more flowers were in bloom, and bird life was steadily increasing. In the bushes by the streams the handsome white-crowned sparrows and green-tailed towhees were in full song, making attractive music; although the song of neither can rightly be compared in point of plaintive beauty with that of the white-throated sparrow, which, except some of the thrushes, and perhaps the winter wren, is the sweetest singer of the Northeastern forests. The spurred towhees were very plentiful; and one morning a willow-thrush sang among the willows like a veery. Both the crested jays and the Woodhouse jays came around camp. Lower down the Western meadow larks were singing beautifully, and vesper finches were abundant. Say's flycatcher, a very attractive bird, with pretty, soft-colored plumage, continually uttering a plaintive single note, and sometimes a warbling twitter, flitted about in the neighborhood of the little log ranch houses. Gangs of blackbirds visited the corrals. I saw but one song sparrow, and curiously enough, though I think it was merely an individual peculiarity, this particular bird had a song entirely different from any I have heard from the familiar Eastern bird—always a favorite of mine.

While up in the mountains hunting, we twice came upon owls, which were rearing their families in the deserted nests of the red-tailed hawk. One was a long-eared owl, and the other a great horned owl, of the pale Western variety. Both were astonishingly tame, and we found it difficult to make them leave their nests, which were in the tops of cottonwood trees.

On the last day we rode down to where Glenwood Springs lies, hemmed in by lofty mountain chains, which are riven in sunder by sheer-sided, cliff-walled canyons. As we left ever farther behind us the wintry desolation of our high hunting grounds we rode into full spring. The green of the valley was a delight to the eye; bird songs sounded on every side, from the fields and from the trees and bushes beside the brooks and irrigation ditches; the air was sweet with the spring-time breath of many budding things. The sarvice bushes were white with bloom, like shadblow on the Hudson; the blossoms of the Oregon grape made yellow mats on the ground. We saw the chunky Say's ground squirrel, looking like a big chipmunk, with on each side a conspicuous white stripe edged with black. In one place we saw quite a large squirrel, grayish, with red on the lower back. I suppose it was only a pine squirrel, but it looked like one of the gray squirrels of southern Colorado. Mountain mockers and the handsome, bold Arkansaw king birds were numerous. The black-tail sage sparrow was conspicuous in the sagebrush, and high among the cliffs the white-throated swifts were soaring. There were numerous warblers, among which I could only make out the black-throated gray, Audubon's, and McGillivray's. In Glenwood Springs itself the purple finches, house finches, and Bullock's orioles were in full song. Flocks of siskins passed with dipping flight. In one rapid little stream we saw a water ousel. Hummingbirds – I suppose the broad-tailed – were common, and as they flew they made, intermittently and almost rhythmically, a curious metallic sound; seemingly it was done with their wings.

But the thing that interested me most in the way of bird life was something I saw in Denver. To my delight I found that the huge hotel at which we took dinner was monopolized by the pretty, musical house finches, to the exclusion of the ordinary city sparrows. The latter are all too plentiful in Denver, as in every other city, and, as always, are noisy, quarrelsome – in short, thoroughly unattractive and disreputable. The house finch, on the contrary, is attractive in looks, in song, and in ways. It was delightful to hear the males singing, often on the wing. They went right up to the top stories of the high hotel, and nested under the eaves and in the cornices. The cities of the Southwestern states are to be congratulated on having this spirited, attractive little songster as a familiar dweller around their houses and in their gardens.

Listening for the pack in Louisiana. Courtesy of the Theodore Roosevelt
Collection, Harvard College Library.

In the Louisiana Canebreaks

Chapter XII

In October, 1907, I spent a fortnight in the canebrakes of northern Louisiana, my hosts being Messrs. John M. Parker and John A. McIlhenny. Surgeon-General Rixey, of the United States Navy, and Dr. Alexander Lambert were with me. I was especially anxious to kill a bear in these canebrakes after the fashion of the old southern planters, who for a century past have followed the bear with horse and hound and horn in Louisiana, Mississippi and Arkansas.

Our first camp was on Tensas Bayou. This is in the heart of the great alluvial bottom-land created during the countless ages through which the mighty Mississippi has poured out of the heart of the continent. It is in the black belt of the South, in which the negroes outnumber the whites four or five to one, the disproportion in the region in which I was actually hunting being far greater. There is no richer soil in all the earth; and when, as will soon be the case, the chances of disaster from flood are over, I believe the whole land will be cultivated and densely peopled. At present the possibility of such flood is a terrible deterrent to settlement, for when the Father of Waters breaks his boundaries he turns the country for a breadth of eighty miles into one broad river, the plantations throughout all this vast extent being from five to twenty feet under water. Cotton is the staple industry, corn also being grown, while there are a few rice fields and occasional small patches of sugar cane. The plantations are for the most part of large size and tilled by negro tenants for the white owners. Conditions are still in some respects like those of the pioneer days. The magnificent forest growth which covers the land is of little value because of the difficulty in getting the trees to market, and the land is actually worth more after the timber has been removed than before. In consequence, the larger trees are often killed by girdling, where the work of felling them would entail disproportionate cost and labor. At dusk, with the sunset glimmering in the west, or in the brilliant moonlight when the moon is full, the cottonfields have a strange spectral look, with the dead trees raising aloft their naked branches. The cottonfields themselves, when the bolls burst open, seem almost as if whitened by snow; and the red and white flowers, interspersed among the burst-open pods, make the whole field beautiful. The rambling one-story houses, surrounded by outbuildings, have a picturesqueness all their own; their very looks betoken the lavish, whole-hearted, generous hospitality of the planters who dwell therein.

Beyond the end of cultivation towers the great forest. Wherever the water stands in pools, and by the edges of the lakes and bayous, the giant cypress loom aloft, rivalled in size by some of the red gums and white oaks. In stature, in towering majesty, they are unsurpassed by any trees of our eastern forests; lordlier kings of the green-leaved world are not to be found until we reach the sequoias and redwoods of the Sierras. Among them grow many other trees—hackberry, thorn, honey locust, tupelo, pecan and ash. In the cypress sloughs the singular knees of the trees stand two or three feet above the black ooze. Palmettos grow thickly in places. The canebrakes stretch along the slight rises of ground, often extending for miles, forming one of the most striking and interesting features of the country. They choke out other growths, the feathery, graceful canes standing in ranks, tall, slender, serried, each but a few inches from his brother, and springing to a height of fifteen or twenty feet. They look like bamboos; they are well-nigh impenetrable to a man on horseback; even on foot they make difficult walking unless free use is made of the heavy bush-knife. It is impossible to see through them for more than fifteen or twenty paces, and often for not half that distance. Bears make their lairs in them, and they are the refuge for hunted things. Outside of them, in the swamp, bushes of many kinds grow thick among the tall trees, and vines and creepers climb the trunks and hang in trailing festoons from the branches. Here, likewise, the bush-knife is in constant play, as the skilled horsemen thread their way, often at a gallop, in and out among the great tree trunks, and through the dense, tangled, thorny undergrowth.

In the lakes and larger bayous we saw alligators and garfish; and monstrous snapping turtles, fearsome brutes of the slime, as heavy as a man, and with huge horny beaks that with a single snap could take off a man's hand or foot. One of the planters with us had lost part of his hand by the bite of an alligator; and had seen a companion seized by the foot by a huge garfish from which he was rescued with the utmost difficulty by his fellow swimmers. There were black bass in the waters, too, and they gave us many a good meal. Thick-bodied water moccasins, foul and dangerous, kept near the water; and farther back in the swamp we found and killed rattlesnakes and copperheads.

Coon and 'possum were very plentiful and in the streams there were minks and a few otters. Black squirrels barked in the tops of the tall trees or descended to the ground to gather nuts or gnaw the shed deer antlers – the latter a habit they shared with the wood rats. To me the most interesting of the smaller mammals, however, were the swamp rabbits, which are thoroughly amphibious in their habits, not only swimming but diving, and taking to the water almost as freely as if they were muskrats. They lived in the depths of the woods and beside the lonely bayous.

Birds were plentiful. Mocking-birds abounded in the clearings, where, among many sparrows of more common kind, I saw the painted finch, the gaudily colored brother of our little indigo bunting, though at this season his plumage was faded and dim. In the thick woods where we hunted there were many cardinal birds and winter wrens, both in full song. Thrashers were even more common; but so cautious that it was rather difficult to see them, in spite of their incessant clucking and calling and their occasional bursts of song. There were crowds of warblers and vireos of many different kinds, evidently migrants from the North, and generally silent. The most characteristic birds, however, were the woodpeckers, of which there were seven or eight species, the commonest around our camp being the handsome red-bellied, the brother of the red-head which we saw in the clearings. The most notable birds and those which most interested me were the great ivory-billed woodpeckers. Of these I saw three, all of them in groves of giant cypress; their brilliant white bills contrasted finely with the black of their general plumage. They were noisy but wary, and they seemed to me to set off the wildness of the swamp as much as any of the beasts of the chase. Among the birds of prey the commonest were the barred owls, which I have never elsewhere found so plentiful. Their hooting and yelling were heard all around us throughout the night, and once one of them hooted at intervals for several minutes at mid-day. One of these owls had caught and was devouring a snake in the late afternoon, while it was still daylight. In the dark nights and still mornings and evenings their cries seemed strange and unearthly, the long hoots varied by screeches, and by all kinds of uncanny noises.

At our first camp our tents were pitched by the bayou. For four days the weather was hot, with steaming rains; after that it grew cool and clear. Huge biting flies, bigger than bees, attacked our horses; but the insect plagues, so veritable a scourge in this country during the months of warm weather, had well-nigh vanished in the first few weeks of the fall.

The morning after we reached camp we were joined by Ben Lilly, the hunter, a spare, full-bearded man, with wild, gentle, blue eyes and a frame of steel and whipcord. I never met any other man so indifferent to fatigue and hardship. He equalled Cooper's Deerslayer in woodcraft, in hardihood, in simplicity—and also in loquacity. The morning he joined us in camp, he had come on foot through the thick woods, followed by his two dogs, and had neither eaten nor drunk for twenty-four hours; for he did not like to drink the swamp water. It had rained hard throughout the night and he had no shelter, no rubber coat, nothing but the clothes he was wearing, and the ground was too wet for him to lie on; so he perched in a crooked tree in the beating rain, much as if he had been a wild turkey. But he was not in the least tired when he struck camp; and, though he slept an hour after breakfast, it was chiefly because he had nothing else to do, inasmuch as it was Sunday, on which day he never hunted nor labored. He could run through the woods like a buck, was far more enduring, and quite as indifferent to weather, though he was over fifty years old. He had trapped and hunted throughout almost all the half century of his life, and on trail of game he was as sure as his own hounds. His observations on wild creatures were singularly close and accurate. He was particularly fond of the chase of the bear, which he followed by himself, with one or two dogs; often he would be on the trail of his quarry for days at a time, lying down to sleep wherever night overtook him; and he had killed over a hundred and twenty bears.

Late in the evening of the same day we were joined by two gentlemen, to whom we owed the success of our hunt. They were Messrs. Clive and Harley Metcalf, planters from Mississippi, men in the prime of life, thorough woodsmen and hunters, skilled marksmen, and utterly fearless horsemen. For a quarter of a century they had hunted bear and deer with horse and hound, and were masters of the art. They brought with them their pack of bear hounds, only one, however, being a thoroughly staunch and seasoned veteran. The pack was under the immediate control of a negro hunter, Holt Collier, in his own way as remarkable a character as Ben Lilley. He was a man of sixty and could neither read nor write, but he had all the dignity of an African chief, and for half a century he had been a bear hunter, having killed or assisted in killing over three thousand bears. He had been born a slave on the Hinds plantation, his father, an old man when he was born, having been the body-servant and cook of "old General Hinds," as he called him, when the latter fought under Jackson at New Orleans. When ten years old Holt had been taken on the horse behind his young master, the Hinds of that day, on a bear hunt, when he killed his first bear. In the Civil War he had not only followed his master to battle as his body-servant, but had acted under him as sharpshooter against the Union soldiers. After the war he continued to stay with his master until the latter died, and had then been adopted by the Metcalfs; and he felt that he had brought them up, and treated them with that mixture of affection and grumbling respect which an old nurse shows toward the lad who has ceased being a child. The two Metcalfs and Holt understood one another thoroughly, and understood their hounds and the game their hounds followed almost as thoroughly.

They had killed many deer and wildcat, and now and then a panther; but their favorite game was the black bear, which, until within a very few years, was extraordinarily plentiful in the swamps and canebrakes on both sides of the lower Mississippi, and which is still found here and there, although in greatly diminished numbers. In Louisiana and Mississippi the bears go into their dens toward the end of January, usually in hollow trees, often very high up in living trees, but often also in great logs that lie rotting on the ground. They come forth toward the end of April, the cubs having been born in the interval. At this time the bears are nearly as fat, so my informants said, as when they enter their dens in January; but they lose their fat very rapidly. On first coming out in the spring they usually eat ash buds and the tender young cane called mutton cane, and at that season they generally refuse to eat the acorns even when they are plentiful. According to my informants it is at this season that they are most apt to take to killing stock, almost always the hogs which run wild or semi-wild in the woods. They are very individual in their habits, however; many of them never touch stock, while others, usually old he-bears, may kill numbers of hogs; in one case an old he-bear began this hog killing just as soon as he left his den. In the summer months they find but little to eat, and it is at this season that they are most industrious in hunting for grubs, insects, frogs and small mammals. In some neighborhoods they do not eat fish, while in other places, perhaps not far away, they not only greedily eat dead fish, but will themselves kill fish if they can find them in shallow pools left by the receding

The bear hunters. Courtesy of the Theodore Roosevelt Collection, Harvard College Library.

waters. As soon as the mast is on the ground they begin to feed upon it, and when the acorns and pecans are plentiful they eat nothing else, though at first berries of all kinds and grapes are eaten also. When in November they have begun only to eat the acorns they put on fat as no other wild animal does, and by the end of December a full-grown bear may weigh at least twice as much as it does in August, the difference being as great as between a very fat and a lean hog. Old he-bears which in August weigh three hundred pounds and upwards will, toward the end of December, weigh six hundred pounds, and even more in exceptional cases.

Bears vary greatly in their habits in different localities, in addition to the individual variation among those of the same neighborhood. Around Avery Island, John McIlhenny's plantation, the bears only appear from June to November; there they never kill hogs, but feed at first on corn and then on sugar-cane, doing immense damage in the fields, quite as much as hogs would do. But when we were on the Tensas we visited a family of settlers who lived right in the midst of the forest ten miles from any neighbors; and although bears were plentiful around them they never molested their corn-fields—in which the coons, however, did great damage.

A big bear is cunning, and is a dangerous fighter to the dogs. It is only in exceptional cases, however, that these black bears, even when wounded and at bay, are dangerous to men, in spite of their formidable strength. Each of the hunters with whom I was camped had been charged by one or two among the scores or hundreds of bears he had slain, but no one of them had ever been injured, although they knew other men who had been injured. Their immunity was due to their own skill and coolness; for when the dogs were around the bear the hunter invariably ran close in so as to kill the bear at once and save the pack. Each of the Metcalfs had on one occasion killed a large bear with a knife, when the hounds had seized it and the men dared not fire for fear of shooting one of them. They had in their younger days hunted with a General Hamberlin, a Mississippi planter whom they well knew, who was then already an old man. He was passionately addicted to the chase of the bear, not only because of the sport it afforded, but also in a certain way as a matter of vengeance; for his father, also a keen bear-hunter, had been killed by a bear. It was an old he, which he had wounded and which had been bayed by the dogs; it attacked him, throwing him down and biting him so severely that he died a couple of days later. This was in 1847. Mr. W. H. Lambeth sends the following account of the fatal encounter:

"I send you an extract from the 'Brother Jonathan,' published in New York in 1847:

" 'Dr. Monroe Hamberlin, Robert Wilson, Joe Brazeil, and others left Satartia, Miss., and in going up Big Sunflower River, met Mr. Leiser and his party of hunters returning to Vicksburg. Mr. Leiser told Dr. Hamberlin that he saw the largest bear track at the big Mound on Lake George that he ever saw, and was afraid to tackle him. Dr. Hamberlin said, "I never saw one that I was afraid to tackle." Dr. Hamberlin landed his skiff at the Mound and his dogs soon bayed the bear. Dr. Hamberlin fired and the ball glanced on the bear's head. The bear caught him by the right thigh and tore all the flesh off. He drew his knife and the bear crushed his right arm. He cheered the dogs and they pulled the bear off. The bear whipped the dogs and attacked him the third time, biting him in the hollow back of his neck. Mr. Wilson came up and shot the bear dead on Dr. Hamberlin. The party returned to Satartia, but Dr. Hamberlin told them to put the bear in the skiff, that he would not leave without his antagonist. The bear weighed 640 pounds.'

"Dr. Hamberlin lived three days. I knew all the parties. His son John and myself hunted with them in 1843 and 1844, when we were too small to carry a gun."

A large bear is not afraid of dogs, and an old he, or a she with cubs, is always on the lookout for a chance to catch and kill any dog that comes near enough. While lean and in good running condition it is not an easy matter to bring a bear to bay; but as they grow fat they become steadily less able to run, and the young ones, and even occasionally a full-grown she, will then readily tree. If a man is not near by, a big bear that has become tired will treat the pack with whimsical indifference. The Metcalfs recounted to me how they had once seen a bear, which had been chased quite a time, evidently make up its mind that it needed a rest and could afford to take it without much regard for the hounds. The bear accordingly selected a small opening and lay flat on its back with its nose and all its four legs extended. The dogs surrounded it in frantic excitement, barking and baying, and gradually coming in a ring very close up. The bear was watching, however, and suddenly sat up with a jerk, frightening the dogs nearly into fits. Half of them turned back-somer-saults in their panic, and all promptly gave the bear ample room. The bear having looked about, lay flat on its back again, and the pack gradually regaining courage once more closed in. At first the bear, which was evidently reluctant to arise, kept them at a distance by now and then thrusting an unexpected paw toward them; and when they became too bold it sat up with a jump and once more put them all to flight.

For several days we hunted perseveringly around this camp on the Tensas Bayou, but without success. Deer abounded, but we could find no bear; and of the deer we killed only what we actually needed for use in camp. I killed one myself by a good shot, in which, however, I fear that the element of luck played a considerable part. We had started as usual by sunrise, to be gone all day; for we never counted upon returning to camp before sunset. For an hour or two we threaded our way, first along an indistinct trail, and then on an old disused road, the hardy woods-horses keeping on a running walk without much regard to the difficulties of the ground. The disused road lay right across a great canebrake, and while some of the party went around the cane with the dogs, the rest of us strung out along the road so as to get a shot at any bear that might come across it. I was following Harley Metcalf, with John McIlhenny and Dr. Rixey behind on the way to their posts, when we heard in the far-off distance two of the younger hounds, evidently on the trail of a deer. Almost immediately afterward a crash in the bushes at our right hand and behind us made me turn around, and I saw a deer running across the few feet of open space; and as I leaped from my horse it disappeared in the cane. I am a rather deliberate shot, and under any circumstances a rifle is not the best weapon for snap shooting, while there is no kind of shooting more difficult than on running game in a canebrake. Luck favored me in this instance, however, for there was a spot a little ahead of where the deer entered in which the cane was thinner, and I kept my rifle on its indistinct, shadowy outline until it reached this spot; it then ran quartering away from me, which made my shot much easier, although I could only catch its general outline through the cane. But the 45-70 which I was using is a powerful gun and shoots right through cane or bushes; and as soon as I pulled the trigger the deer, with a bleat, turned a tremendous somersault and was dead when we reached it. I was not a little pleased that my bullet should have sped so true when I was making my first shot in company with my hard-riding straight-shooting planter friends.

But no bear were to be found. We waited long hours on likely stands. We rode around the canebrakes through the swampy jungle, or threaded our way across them on trails cut by the heavy wood-knives of my companions; but we found nothing. Until the trails were cut the canebrakes were impenetrable to a horse and were difficult enough to a man on foot. On going through them it seemed as if we must be in the tropics; the silence, the stillness, the heat, and the obscurity, all combining to give a certain eeriness to the task, as we chopped our winding way slowly through the dense mass of close-growing, featherfronded stalks. Each of the hunters prided himself on his skill with the horn, which was an essential adjunct of the hunt, used both to summon and control the hounds, and for signalling among the hunters themselves. The tones of many of the horns were full and musical; and it was pleasant to hear them as they wailed to one another, backwards and forwards, across the great stretches of lonely swamp and forest.

A few days convinced us that it was a waste of time to stay longer where we were. Accordingly, early one morning we hunters started for a new camp fifteen or twenty miles to the southward, on Bear Lake. We took the hounds with us, and each man carried what he chose or could in his saddle-pockets, while his slicker was on his horse's back behind him. Otherwise we took absolutely nothing in the way of supplies, and the negroes with the tends and camp equipage were three days before they overtook us. On our way down we were joined by Major Amacker and Dr. Miller, with a small pack of cat hounds. These were good deer dogs, and they ran down and killed on the ground a good-sized bob-cat—a wild-cat, as it is called in the South. It was a male and weighed twenty-three and a half pounds. It had just killed and eaten a large rabbit. The stomachs of the deer we killed, by the way, contained acorns and leaves.

Our new camp was beautifully situated on the bold, steep bank of Bear Lake—a tranquil stretch of water, part of an old river-bed, a couple of hundred yards broad, with a winding length of several miles. Giant cypress grew at the edge of the water; the singular cypress knees rising in every direction round about, while at the bottoms of the trunks themselves were often cavernous hollows opening beneath the surface of water, some of them serving as dens for alligators. There was a waxing moon, so that the nights were as beautiful as the days.

From our new camp we hunted as steadily as from the old. We saw bear sign, but not much of it, and only one or two fresh tracks. One day the hounds jumped a bear, probably a yearling from the way it ran; for at this season a yearling or a two-year-old will run almost like a deer, keeping to the thick cane as long as it can and then bolting across through the bushes of the ordinary swamp land until it can reach another canebrake. After a three hours' run this particular animal managed to get clear away without one of the hunters ever seeing it, and it ran until all the dogs were tired out. A day or two afterwards one of the other members of the party shot a small yearling—that is, a bear which would have been two years old in the following February. It was very lean, weighing but fifty-five pounds. The finely-chewed acorns in its stomach showed that it was already beginning to find mast.

We had seen the tracks of an old she in the neighborhood, and the next morning we started to hunt her out. I went with Clive Metcalf. We had been joined overnight by Mr. Ichabod Osborn and his son Tom, two Louisiana planters, with six or eight hounds—or rather bear dogs, for in these packs most of the animals are of mixed blood, and, as with all packs that are used in the genuine hunting of the wilderness, pedigree counts for nothing as compared with steadiness, courage and intelligence. There were only two of the new dogs that were really staunch bear dogs. The father of Ichabod Osborn had taken up the plantation upon which they were living in 1811, only a few years after Louisiana became part of the United States, and young Osborn was now the third in line from father to son who had steadily hunted bears in this immediate neighborhood.

On reaching the cypress slough near which the tracks of the old she had been seen the day before, Clive Metcalf and I separated from the others and rode off at a lively pace between two of the canebrakes. After an hour or two's wait we heard, very far off, the notes of one of the loudest-mouthed hounds, and instantly rode toward it, until we could make out the babel of the pack. Some hard galloping brought us opposite the point toward which they were heading—for experienced hunters can often tell the probable line of a bear's flight, and the spots at which it will break cover. But on this occasion the bear shied off from leaving the thick cane and doubled back; and soon the hounds were once more out of hearing, while we galloped desperately around the edge of the cane. The tough woods-horses kept their feet like cats as they leaped logs, plunged through bushes, and dodged in and out among the tree trunks; and we had all we could do to prevent the vines from lifting us out of the saddle, while the thorns tore our hands and faces. Hither and thither we went, now at a trot, now at a run, now stopping to listen for the pack. Occasionally we could hear the hounds, and then off we would go racing through the forest toward the point for which we thought they were heading. Finally, after a couple of hours of this, we came up on one side of a canebrake on the other side of which we could hear, not only the pack, but the yelling and cheering of Harley Metcalf and Tom Osborn and one or two of the negro hunters, all of whom were trying to keep the dogs up to their work in the thick cane. Again we rode ahead, and now in a few minutes were rewarded by hearing the leading dogs come to bay in the thickest of the cover. Having galloped as near to the spot as we could we threw ourselves off the horses and plunged into the cane, trying to cause as little disturbance as possible, but of course utterly unable to avoid making some noise. Before we were within gunshot, however, we could tell by the sounds that the bear had once again started, making what is called a "walking bay." Clive Metcalf, a finished bear-hunter, was speedily able to determine what the bear's probable course would be, and we stole through the cane until we came to a spot near which he thought the quarry would pass. Then we crouched down, I with my rifle at the ready. Nor did we have long to wait. Peering through the thick-growing stalks I suddenly made out the dim outline of the bear coming straight toward us; and noiselessly I cocked and half-raised my rifle, waiting for a clearer chance. In a few seconds it came; the bear turned almost broadside to me, and walked forward very stiff-legged, almost as if on tiptoe, now and then looking back at the nearest dogs. These were two in number—Rowdy, a very deep-voiced hound, in the lead, and Queen, a shrill-tongued brindled bitch, a little behind. Once or twice the bear paused as she looked back at them, evidently hoping that they would come so near that by a sudden race she could catch one of them. But they were too wary.

All of this took but a few moments, and as I saw the bear quite distinctly some twenty yards off, I fired for behind the shoulder. Although I could see her outline, yet the cane was so thick that my sight was on it and not on the bear itself. But I knew my bullet would go true; and, sure enough, at the crack of the rifle the bear stumbled and fell forward, the bullet having passed through both lungs and out at the opposite side. Immediately the dogs came running forward at full speed, and we raced forward likewise lest the pack should receive damage. The bear had but a minute or two to live, yet even in that time more than one valuable hound might lose its life; so when within half a dozen steps of the black, angered beast, I fired again, breaking the spine at the root of the neck; and down went the bear stark dead, slain in the canebrake in true hunter fashion. One by one the hounds struggled up and fell on their dead quarry, the noise of the worry filling the air. Then we dragged the bear out to the edge of the cane, and my companion wound his horn to summon the other hunters.

This was a big she-bear, very lean, and weighing two hundred and two pounds. In her stomach were palmetto berries, beetles and a little mutton cane, but chiefly acorns chewed up in a fine brown mass.

John McIlhenny had killed a she-bear about the size of this on his plantation at Avery's Island the previous June. Several bear had been raiding his corn-fields, and one evening he determined to try to waylay them. After dinner he left the ladies of his party on the gallery of his house while he rode down in a hollow and concealed himself on the lower side of the corn-field. Before he had waited ten minutes a she-bear and her cub came into the field. There she rose on her hind legs, tearing down an armful of ears of corn which she seemingly gave to the cub, and then rose for another armful. McIlhenny shot her; tried in vain to catch the cub; and rejoined the party on the veranda, having been absent but one hour.

After the death of my bear I had only a couple of days left. We spent them a long distance from camp, having to cross two bayous before we got to the hunting grounds. I missed a shot at a deer, seeing little more than the flicker of its white tail through the dense bushes; and the pack caught and killed a very lean two-year-old bear weighing eighty pounds. Near a beautiful pond called Panther Lake we found a deer-lick, the ground not merely bare, but furrowed into hollows by the tongues of the countless generations of deer that had frequented the place. We also passed a huge mound, the only hillock in the entire district; it was the work of man, for it had been built in the unknown past by those unknown people whom we call mound-builders. On the trip, all told, we killed and brought into camp three bear, six deer, a wildcat, a turkey, a possum and a dozen squirrels; and we ate everything except the wildcat.

In the evenings we sat around the blazing campfires, and, as always on such occasions, each hunter told tales of his adventures and of the strange feats and habits of the beasts of the wilderness. There had been beaver all through this delta in the old days, and a very few are still left in out-of-the-way places. One Sunday morning we saw two wolves, I think young of the year, appear for a moment on the opposite side of the bayou, but they vanished before we could shoot. All of our party had had a good deal of experience with wolves. The Metcalfs had had many sheep killed by them, the method of killing being invariably by a single bite which tore open the throat while the wolf ran beside his victim. The wolves also killed young hogs, but were very cautious about meddling with an old sow; while one of the big half-wild boars that ranged free through the woods had no fear of any number of wolves. Their endurance and the extremely difficult nature of the country made it difficult to hunt them, and the hunters all bore them a grudge, because if a hound got lost in a region where wolves were at all plentiful they were almost sure to find and kill him before he got home. They were fond of preying on dogs, and at times would boldly kill the hounds right ahead of the hunters. In one instance, while the dogs were following a bear and were but a couple of hundred yards in front of the horsemen, a small party of wolves got in on them and killed two. One of the Osborns, having a valuable hound which was addicted to wandering in the woods, saved him from the wolves by putting a bell on him. The wolves evidently suspected a trap and would never go near the dog. On one occasion another of his hounds got loose with a chain on, and they found him a day or two afterwards unharmed, his chain having become entangled in the branches of a bush. One or two wolves had evidently walked around and around the imprisoned dog, but the chain had awakened their suspicions and they had not pounced on him. They had killed a yearling heifer a short time before, on Osborn's plantation, biting her in the hams. It has been my experience that fox hounds as a rule are afraid of attacking a wolf; but all of my friends assured me that their dogs, if a sufficient number of them were together, would tackle a wolf without hesitation; the packs, however, were always composed, to the extent of at least half, of dogs which, though part hound, were part shepherd or bull or some other breed. Dr. Miller had hunted in Arkansas with a pack specially trained after the wolf. There were twenty-eight of them all told, and on this hunt they ran down and killed unassisted four full-grown wolves, although some of the hounds were badly cut. None of my companions had ever known of wolves actually molesting men, but Mr. Ichabod Osborn's son-in-law had a queer adventure with wolves while riding alone through the woods one late afternoon. His horse acting nervously, he looked about and saw that five wolves were coming towards him. One was a bitch, the other four were males. They seemed to pay little heed to him, and he shot one of the males, which crawled off. The next minute the bitch ran straight toward him and was almost at his stirrup when he killed her. The other three wolves, instead of running away, jumped to and fro growling, with their hair bristling, and he killed two of them; whereupon the survivor at last made off. He brought the scalps of the three dead wolves home with him.

Near our first camp was the carcass of a deer, a yearling buck, which had been killed by a cougar. When first found, the wounds on the carcass showed that the deer had been killed by a bite in the neck at the back of the head; but there were scratches on the rump as if the panther had landed on its back. One of the negro hunters, Brutus Jackson, evidently a trustworthy man, told me that he had twice seen cougars, each time under unexpected conditions.

Once he saw a bobcat race up a tree, and riding toward it saw a panther reared up against the trunk. The panther looked around at him quite calmly, and then retired in leisurely fashion. Jackson went off to get some hounds, and when he returned two hours afterwards the bobcat was still up the tree, evidently so badly scared that he did not wish to come down. The hounds were unable to follow the cougar. On another occasion he heard a tremendous scuffle and immediately afterwards saw a big doe racing along with a small cougar literally riding it. The cougar was biting the neck, but low down near the shoulders; he was hanging on with his front paws, but was tearing away with his hind claws, so that the deer's hair appeared to fill the air. As soon as Jackson appeared the panther left the deer. He shot it, and the doe galloped off, apparently without serious injury.

APPENDIX

Some Notes on Bear Interactions with Other Game

ELK

The elk has other foes besides man. The grizzly will always make a meal of one if he gets a chance; and against his ponderous weight and savage prowess hoofs and antlers avail but little. Still he is too clumsy and easily avoided ever to do very much damage in the herds.

from Hunting Trips of a Ranchman, *1885, p. 275.*

However, the fiercest wapiti bull, when in a wild state, flees the neighborhood of man with the same panic terror shown by the cows; and he makes no stand against a grizzly, though when his horns are grown he has little fear of either wolf or cougar if on his guard and attacked fairly.

from The Wilderness Hunter, *1904 edition, Vol. 1, p. 191.*

MOOSE

I had been told by old hunters that black bears would sometimes attack moose calves, and in one instance, in the Rockies, my informant described to me how a big grizzly, but a few weeks out of its den in spring, attacked and slew full-grown moose. I was not surprised at the latter statement, having myself come across cattle-killing grizzlies; but I wondered at a black bear, which is not much of a beast of prey, venturing to meddle with the young of so formidable a fighter as a moose. However, it is true. Recently my nephew Hall Roosevelt, who was working at Dawson City, went on a moose hunt in the valley of the Yukon. One night a moose cow passed by the camp, having first swum a stream in front of the camp. She was followed at some little distance by a calf. The latter halted near the camp. Suddenly a black bear, with a tremendous crashing of branches, came with a rush through the bushes, and seized the calf; although it was driven off, it had with its teeth so injured the spine of the calf that they were obliged to shoot the latter.

from A Book Lover's Holiday in the Open, *1920 edition, Appendix A, p. 359.*

BIGHORN
SHEEP

*Generally the band is led by a ewe; but in a case of immediate
and pressing danger the ram assumes the head-ship. Aside from man,
mountain sheep have fewer foes than most other game. Bears are too clumsy
to catch them; and lynx and fox, inveterate enemies of fawns, rarely get
up to the high, breezy nurseries of the young lambs.*

from Ranch Life and the Hunting
Trail, *1906 edition, p. 254.*

BISON

But one beast of prey existed sufficiently powerful to conquer it when full grown and in health; and this, the grizzly bear, could only be considered an occasional foe. The Indians were its most dangerous enemies, but they were without horses, and their weapons, bows and arrows, were only available at close range; so that a slight degree of speed enabled buffalo to get out of the way of their human foes when discovered, and on the open plains a moderate development of the senses was sufficient to warn them of the approach of the latter before they had come up to the very close distance required for their primitive weapons to take effect. Thus the strength, size, and gregarious habits of the brute were sufficient for a protection against most foes; and a slight degree of speed and moderate development of the senses served as adequate guards against the grizzlies and bow-bearing foot Indians. Concealment and the habit of seeking lonely and remote places for a dwelling would have been of no service.

from Hunting Trips of a Ranchman,
1885, pp. 245–246.

COUGAR

When hungry, a cougar will attack any thing it can master. I have known of their killing wolves and large dogs. A friend of mine, a ranchman in Wyoming, had two grizzly bear cubs in his possession at one time, and they were kept in a pen outside the ranch. One night two cougars came down, and after vain efforts to catch a dog which was on the place, leaped into the pen and carried off the two young bears!

from Hunting Trips of a Ranchman, *1885, p. 27.*

. . . cougar attacking the grizzly bear. Here I am on ground that I do know. It is true that an occasional old hunter asserts that the cougar does this, but the old hunter who makes such an assertion also invariably insists that the cougar is a ferocious and habitual man-killer, and the two statements rest upon equally slender foundations of fact. I have never yet heard of a single authentic instance of a cougar interfering with a full-grown bear. It will kill bear cubs if it gets a chance; but then so will the fox and the fisher, not to speak of the wolf. In 1894, a cougar killed a colt on a brushy river bottom a dozen miles below my ranch on the Little Missouri. I went down to visit the carcass and found that it had been taken possession of by a large grizzly. Both I and the hunter who was with me were very much interested in what had occurred, and after a careful examination of the tracks we concluded that the bear had arrived on the second night after the kill. He had feasted heartily on the remains, while the cougar, whose tracks were evident here and there at a little distance from the carcass, had seemingly circled around it, and had certainly not interfered with the bear, or even ventured to approach him. Now, if a cougar would ever have meddled with a large bear it would surely have been on such an occasion as this.

from Outdoor Pastimes of an American Hunter, *1925 edition, pp. 21–22.*

Appendix

There is no kind of game, save the full-grown grizzly and buffalo, which it does not at times assail and master. It readily snaps up grizzly cubs or buffalo calves; and in at least one instance, I have known of it springing on, slaying, and eating a full-grown wolf. I presume the latter was taken by surprise. On the other hand, the cougar itself has to fear the big timber wolves when maddened by the winter hunger and gathered in small parties; while a large grizzly would of course be an overmatch for it twice over, though its superior agility puts it beyond the grizzly's power to harm it, unless by some unlucky chance taken in a cave.

from The Wilderness Hunter, *1893.*

NOTES TO INTRODUCTION

1. Paul Cutright, *Theodore Roosevelt the Naturalist* (New York: Harper & Brothers, 1956).

2. C. Hart Merriam, "Roosevelt, The Naturalist," *Science*, Vol. 75, No. 1937, February 12, 1932, pp. 182–83.

3. C. Hart Merriam, "Cervus Roosevelti, A New Elk from the Olympics," *Proceedings of the Biological Society of Washington*, Volume XI, December 17, 1897, p. 275.

4. Cutright, p. 54; George Bird Grinnell, "President Roosevelt as a Sportsman," *Forest and Stream*, December 5, 1903, p. 437; Roosevelt himself remarked, in the Appendix to *The Wilderness Hunter*, that "As far as I know, the description in my *Ranch Life* of the habits and the chase of the mountain sheep is the only moderately complete account thereof that has ever been published."

5. Cutright, *Roosevelt the Naturalist*, p. 54.

6. Edmund Heller, "Roosevelt and Wildlife," *Roosevelt Wildlife Bulletin*, Vol. I, No. 1, December, 1921, p. 51.

7. Theodore Roosevelt, *The Wilderness Hunter* (New York: G.P. Putnam's Sons, 1893), p. 265. Roosevelt's fellow Boone and Crockett Club member Archibald Rogers, writing in *American Big Game Hunting* (New York: Forest and Stream Publishing Company, 1893), remarked that "probably more horrible lies have been told by bear-hunters than by any other class of men, except, perhaps, fishermen, who are renowned for their yarns."
Roosevelt believed, with some justification, that he had the best big-game library in the United States. See Frederick Goff, "T.R.'s Big Game Library," *Quarterly Journal of the Library of Congress*, Vol. 21, No. 3, 1964, pp. 166–72.
For an example of thorough scientific description of bears in the mid-1800s see Spencer Fullerton Baird, *United States Pacific Railroad Exploration and Surveys – Zoology – General Report* (Washington: U.S. Government, 1857), pp. 216–28.

8. At various times, Roosevelt waxed eloquent about most species of game. Bighorn sheep were the most physically demanding to hunt, grizzlies were the most dangerous, and so on. In *The Wilderness Hunter* he said that "to me still-hunting elk in the mountains, when they are calling, is one of the most attractive of sports . . . the wapiti is

not only the most stately and beautiful of American game—far more so than the bison and the moose, his only rivals in size—but is also the noblest of the stag kind throughout the world."

It might be worth explaining to the uninitiated that the term "still hunt" did not mean hunting by sitting still. Roosevelt defined it in *Hunting Trips of a Ranchman* (New York: G.P. Putnam's Sons, 1885) on page 160 as "pretty much every kind of chase where a single man, unaided by a dog, and almost always on foot, outgenerals a deer and kills it with a rifle." Of course one could also "still hunt" other game.

9. Elting Morison, ed., *The Letters of Theodore Roosevelt* (Cambridge: Harvard University Press, 1951–1954), I:82.

10. G. Edward White, *The Eastern Establishment and the Western Experience* (New Haven: Yale University Press, 1968), p. 93. White's book is but one of several good sources of information and analysis of Roosevelt's youth and western years. The following are essential reading and also well documented enough to lead you to more detail: Edmund Morris, *The Rise of Theodore Roosevelt* (New York: Random House, 1979), David McCullough, *Mornings on Horseback* (New York: Simon and Schuster, 1981), and Carleton Putnam, *Theodore Roosevelt, The Formative Years* (New York: Charles Scribner's Sons, 1958).

I have not attempted to review Roosevelt's youthful enthusiasm for natural history, his early hunting experiences, or his academic interests in nature; the above titles do so quite exhaustively.

11. Theodore Roosevelt, *An Autobiography* (Charles Scribner's Sons, 1929), pp. 54–55.

12. William Wright, *The Grizzly Bear* (New York: Charles Scribner's Sons, 1909) and *The Black Bear* (New York: Charles Scribner's Sons, 1909).

13. Roosevelt's hunting books were reviewed widely. For summaries of the reviews, see Cutright and Morris, above, as well as Aloysius Norton, *Theodore Roosevelt* (Boston: Twayne Publishers, G.K. Hall & Co., 1980). The Norton book is a study of Roosevelt as a writer.

14. Two good overviews of the early wildlife conservation movement that emphasize sportsmen are John Reiger, *American Sportsmen and the Origins of Conservation* (New York: Winchester Press, 1975) and James Trefethen, *An American Crusade for Wildlife* (New York: Winchester Press, 1975). Both deal extensively with Roosevelt and the Boone and Crockett Club.

Two scholarly examinations of the development of American Wildlife law are Michael Bean, *The Evolution of National Wildlife Law* (Washington: U.S. Government Printing Office, 1978) and Thomas Lund, *American Wildlife Law* (Berkeley: University of California Press, 1980).

15. Morris, p. 286.

16. Roosevelt hardly seems faultless to us now in his treatment of some small animals,

though; he enjoyed occasional target practice, using jackrabbits, and more than once shot at eagles and hawks, which, like jackrabbits, weren't highly thought of in his day. Roosevelt's sensitivity to potential criticism over wasted game shows up in his writings. For example, in *The Wilderness Hunter*, he reported that three bull elk that were killed primarily for trophies were unfit to eat anyway; "the flesh was far too strong to be worth taking, for it was just the height of the rut." Many modern hunters would disagree with him on this point, but Roosevelt was conscious of the need to explain the apparent waste.

17. Perhaps the most famous incident involving Roosevelt's pride in his own sportmanship was the story of the Chicago attorney and sportsman A.L. Trude. For reasons not now clear, in mid-1890s Trude spread a terrible story about Roosevelt having had his trophies shot for him by his guides, having had his big-game photographs rigged, and having only ever really shot one bear, in a trap. See Cutright, pp. 51–52, and Jack Willis, *Roosevelt in the Rough* (New York: Ives Washburn, 1931), pp. 207-11. Roosevelt's response was fast and angry, challenging Trude to prove any of it. Trude's reasons never became clear, but he quickly backed down. Roosevelt's formal public statement on the matter appeared in *Forest and Stream* on November 2, 1895, and because it reveals his feelings about the quantity of game he killed I quote part of it:

> Some of my bear hunting has been done with Willis, and some of it with William Merrifield, of Medora, N.D., who was at the time on my ranch, and some with Hank Griffen, who is dead. Three bears I shot when I was alone. As for shooting elk cows and calves, in all my twelve years' hunting in the west put together I have killed but five, and these were when we were in need of meat. The most successful elk hunt I ever made was in 1891, south of the Yellowstone National Park. I was with old Tazewell Woody, whose address is at Mammoth Hot Springs . . . A full account of the trip is published in my book *The Wilderness Hunter*.

Roosevelt went on to challenge Trude to give the date or place of any of the alleged incidents, and concluded that "Mr. Trude is unfit for membership in any club or association of gentlemen, and is unfit for the acquaintance of any man of honor."

George Bird Grinnell, Editor of *Forest and Stream*, was a co-founder with Roosevelt of the Boone and Crockett Club in 1888, and defended Roosevelt against the charges.

A more specific accounting of game killed was made by Roosevelt in the conclusion of his chapter "An Elk-Hunt at Two-Ocean Pass," in *The Wilderness Hunter*. It gives a good idea of what he considered a reasonably successful hunt, as well as how much such a hunt could vary:

> I have described this hunt at length because, though I enjoyed it particularly on account of the comfort in which we traveled and the beauty of the land, yet, in point of success in finding and killing game, in value of trophies procured, and in its alternations of good and bad luck, it may fairly stand as the type of a dozen such hunts I have made. Twice I have been much more successful; the difference being due to sheer luck, as I hunted equally hard in all three instances. Thus on this trip I killed and saw nothing but elk; yet the other members of the party either saw, or saw fresh signs of, not only blacktail deer, but sheep, bear, bison, moose, cougar, and wolf. Now in 1889 I hunted over almost precisely similar country, only further to the northwest, on the boundary between Idaho and Montana, and, with the exception of sheep, I stumbled on all the animals mentioned, and white goat in addition, so that my bag of twelve head actually included eight species—much the best bag I ever made, and the only one that could really be called out of the common. In 1884, on a trip to the Bighorn Mountains, I killed three bear, six elk, and six deer. In laying in the winter stock of meat for my ranch

Notes to Introduction

I often far excelled these figures as far as mere numbers went; but on no other regular hunting trip, where the quality and not the quantity of the game was the prime consideration, have I ever equalled them; and on several where I worked hardest I hardly averaged a head a week.

On the hunt he had just finished he got nine elk in about two weeks.

18. Edward Wagenknecht, *The Seven Worlds of Theodore Roosevelt* (New York: Longmans, Green & Co., 1958), p. 20.

19. See White, McCullough, and Morris for Roosevelt's romance with the cowboy. Also, see John Barsness, "Theodore Roosevelt as Cowboy: The Virginian as Jacksonian Man," *American Quarterly*, Vol. 21, No. 3, 1969, pp. 609–19.

Roosevelt knew his place in the western scene quite well; he was not deluding himself that he had become a veteran frontiersman overnight. He wrote to his sister in 1884 that "for the last week I have been fulfilling a boyish ambition of mine–that is, I have been playing at frontier hunter with good earnest, having been off entirely alone, with my horse and rifle on the prairie. I wanted to see if I could not do perfectly well without a guide, and I succeeded beyond my expectations" (*Letters From Theodore Roosevelt to Anna Roosevelt Cowles*, New York: Scribners, 1924, p. 59).

20. McCullough, *Mornings on Horseback*, p. 320.

21. See pp. 14–15 for a summing-up of Roosevelt's hunting credo.

22. Audubon, throughout his life, indulged in extraordinary killing of the birds he painted. He, like Roosevelt, must be viewed in the context of his times, but a few examples are illustrative of his excess.

John Chancellor, Audubon's recent biographer (*Audubon*, The Viking Press, New York, 1978), described Audubon's plans on part of an expedition to Florida:

> He wanted to kill twenty-five brown pelicans in order to draw a single male bird. Why he should have needed so many birds for a single drawing is curious. It was partly the fun of killing them at a time when people's thoughts had not turned towards conservation and partly for the sake of giving accurate anatomical descriptions of the species and their individual variations. His friends in England, MacGillivray in particular, were clamoring for as many specimens as possible. [p. 178]

There is no question that Audubon had an unabashed joy of killing. On that same trip, also hunting pelicans, he commented that one day he "would have shot one hundred of there [sic] reverend sirs, had not a mistake taken place in the reloading of my gun" (p. 179). As Chancellor put it, "for Audubon birds were few in number if he shot less than a hundred per day" (p. 179).

Roosevelt's own interest in taxidermy and natural history is probably best portrayed in McCullough's book *Mornings on Horseback*. McCullough takes great pains to portray the great breadth of influences on the young Teddy. For example, Roosevelt's father was a moving force behind the founding of the American Museum of Natural History, and the senior Roosevelt was surrounded by nature enthusiasts and leading scientists.

In his later years, Roosevelt realized, as did many naturalists in the early 1900s, that the old-fashioned collecting techniques were wasteful: "When I was young I fell into the usual fashion of those days and collected 'specimens' industriously, thereby committing an entirely needless butchery of our ordinary birds. I am happy to say that there has been a great change for the better since then in our ways of looking at these things" (Wilson, *Theodore Roosevelt, Outdoorsman,* p. 156).

The excesses of "scientific collecting" outlived Roosevelt by many years. For a good example of a professional zoologist's awakening to the needless waste of such excesses, see Victor Scheffer, *Adventures of a Zoologist* (New York: Charles Scribner's Sons, 1980). Scheffer, a marine biologist, struggled with the problem of excessive collecting in the 1930s and 1940s.

23. Both Reiger and Trefethen, above, recount the work of early sportsmen, pointing out that sportsmen also frequently worked to protect non-game species, such as wading birds and songbirds.

24. A good recent popular overview of the hunter/anti-hunter controversy is John Mitchell, *The Hunt* (New York: Alfred Knopf, 1980), based on a series of articles done for *Audubon* magazine. For a fascinating statistical analysis of present-day attitudes about wildlife and hunting, see the ongoing study by Stephen Kellert, the first part of which was titled "Public Attitudes Toward Critical Wildlife and Natural Habitat Issues" (Washington: U.S. Fish and Wildlife Service, October 15, 1979).

25. Even before he assumed the Vice Presidency the old story of poor sportsmanship, spread in 1895, was dragged out. See, for example, George Bird Grinnell, "Governor Roosevelt's Bear Record," *Forest and Stream,* July 28, 1900, p. 1.

26. The most thorough research into the infamous Mississippi bear hunt has been done by former Curator of the Theodore Roosevelt Collection at Harvard, Gregory Wilson. See Gregory Wilson, "How the Teddy Bear Got His Name," *The Washington Post Potomac,* November 30, 1969, pp. 33–35. Accounts of the hunt included Lindsay Denison, "President Roosevelt's Mississippi Bear Hunt," *Outing,* February, 1903, p. 610, and Orland Armstrong, "He Tracked Bear for Roosevelt," *New York Herald Tribune,* January 3, 1923, and Harris Dickson, "Bear Stories," *Saturday Evening Post,* April 10, 1909, pp. 20–21, 51–52. Among the other interesting sources of information on this hunt are Roosevelt's comments in *Theodore Roosevelt's Letters to His Children* (New York: Charles Scribner's Sons, 1919).

27. It is of interest that there was more than one form of the Berryman cartoon. The most famous one–that is, the most frequently republished one–may not have been the first; see correspondence filed under "Teddy Bear" in the Theodore Roosevelt Collection, Harvard University. It appears that Berryman redrew the picture after it became well known; the version we are now familiar with shows a more robust and respectable-looking Roosevelt than the original, in which his body features are more childlike. The correspondence goes on to suggest the existence of a possible third Berryman variant as well.

28. Wilson, p. 34. A recent book on Teddy Bears is Peter Bull, *The Teddy Bear Book* (New York: Random House, 1970), a whimsical appreciation of this famous toy.

Also of interest is the conflicting story that the original Teddy Bear was named for the German ruler Edward, a contemporary of Roosevelt's.

29. Wilson, p. 34.

30. Seymour Eaton, *The Roosevelt Bears, Their Travels and Adventures* (Philadelphia: Edward Stern & Co., 1906).

Another Roosevelt bear-story, less well known, was told by Roosevelt in *Outdoor Pastimes of an American Hunter* (New York: Charles Scribner's Sons, 1925 edition):

> At different times I have been given a fairly apalling number of animals, from known and unknown friends; in one year the list included—besides a lion, a hyena, and a zebra from the Emperor of Ethiopia—five bears, a wildcat, a coyote, two macaws, an eagle, a barn owl, and several snakes and lizards. Most of these went to the Zoo, but a few were kept by the children. Those thus kept numbered at one end of the scale gentle, trustful, pretty things, like kangaroo rats and flying squirrels; and at the other end a queer-tempered young black bear, which the children named Jonathan Edwards, partly because of certain well-marked Calvinistic tendencies in his disposition, partly out of compliment to their mother, whose ancestors included that Puritan divine . . . The bear added zest to life in more ways than one. When we took him to walk, it was always with a chain and club; and when at last he went to the Zoo, the entire household breathed a sigh of relief, although I think the dogs missed him, as he had occasionally yielded them the pleasure of the chase in its strongest form.

31. Morison, *Letters,* III:387–89.

32. Cutright, pp. 90–93.

33. Morison, *Letters,* III:379.

34. John Burroughs, *Camping and Tramping With Roosevelt* (New York: Houghton Mifflin Co., 1907), pp. 6–7. Burroughs further remarked that the woman "did not know that I was then cherishing the secret hope that I might be allowed to shoot a cougar or a bobcat; but this fun did not come to me."

Both Roosevelt's and Burroughs's full accounts of the Yellowstone visit were reprinted in Paul Schullery, ed., *Old Yellowstone Days* (Boulder: Colorado Associated University Press, 1979). A thorough examination of Roosevelt's involvement with Yellowstone Park is Paul Schullery, "A Partnership in Conservation: Roosevelt and Yellowstone," *Montana, the Magazine of Western History,* Vol. XXVIII, No. 3, July, 1978, pp. 2–15.

35. Schullery, "A Partnership . . . ," p. 6.

36. A.P. news release, January 22, Nashua, New Hampshire, unsigned clipping in the Theodore Roosevelt Collection, Harvard University.

37. DeVoto, Bernard, ed., *Mark Twain in Eruption, Hitherto Unpublished Pages About Men and Events* (New York: Capricorn Books, 1968).

38. Ibid.

39. Roosevelt, *Outdoor Pastimes* (1925 edition), p. 375. Roosevelt returned often to

Notes to Introduction

the topic of the sportsman's responsibility to be a functioning member of society. Take for example the following passage from *African Game Trails*, about the relative worth of trophies:

> A good head is of course better than a poor one; and a special effort to secure an exceptional head is sportsmanlike and proper. But to let the desire for "record" heads, to the exclusion of all else, become a craze, is absurd. The making of such a collection is in itself not only proper but meritorious; all I object to is the loss of all sense of proportion in connection therewith. It is just as with philately, or heraldry, or collecting the signatures of famous men. The study of stamps, or of coats of arms, or the collecting of autographs, is an entirely legitimate amusement, and may be more than a mere amusement; it is only when the student or collector allows himself utterly to misestimate the importance of his pursuit that it becomes ridiculous.

Or, elsewhere in the same volume, his description of the famous hunter Edward North Buxton:

> With Buxton big-game hunting is not a business but a pastime, not allowed to become a mania or in any way interfere with the serious occupations of life, whether public or private; and yet as he has carried it on it is much more than a mere pastime, it is a craft, a pursuit of value in exercising and developing hardihood of body and the virile courage and resolution which necessarily lie at the base of every strong and manly character.

The African expedition is another good example of how historians ridiculed Roosevelt's hunting by taking it out of its context. Emily Hahn ("My Dear Selous," *American Heritage*, April 1963, pp. 40–42, 92–99), discussing the safari, claims that "Roosevelt continued his triumphant way, shooting practically everything that moved and collecting so much that the museum respectfully but firmly refused to put it all on view. Fifty specimens *only*, said the authorities, were what they had room for." This casual jab implies that Roosevelt killed far more animals than the Smithsonian wanted, but consider the following figures. Roosevelt and his son, Kermit, killed a total of 512 animals, including small game and birds. Of these, they kept "about a dozen" as trophies. The rest went to the Smithsonian. The *total* take of the safari, on the other hand, was over *11,000* specimens, including 4,897 mammals, 4,000 birds, 500 fishes, and 2,000 reptiles. Practically all of the specimens taken on the safari were taken by the Smithsonian naturalists. Roosevelt and his son accounted for less than five percent of the take.

Most museums store far more than they exhibit, and certainly most of what the naturalists collected was intended to become a "study collection," not exhibited but preserved and used for research. If the Smithsonian had to refuse to exhibit some of Roosevelt's trophies, it must have been because they lacked room, not because they did not want to have the trophies.

40. A good review of these changing attitudes is James Turner, *Reckoning With the Beast: Animals, Pain, and Humanity in the Victorian Mind* (Baltimore: Johns Hopkins University Press, 1980).

41. Topsell, E., *The History of Four-footed Beasts* (New York: Da Capo Press, 1967), 3 vols., unabridged republication of the 1658 edition. Topsell was based mostly on earlier writers, his text being largely quotations and paraphrases of them.

42. The subject of bear denning has been closely examined by scientists in the past

twenty years. For quite a long time, scientists hesitated to call the bear a true hibernator, because bears do not slip into the coma-like sleep of many other hibernators. Bears are easily roused, and though their bodily processes are greatly slowed by hibernation, they can be roused quickly. See Paul Schullery, *The Bears of Yellowstone* (Yellowstone Park: The Yellowstone Library and Museum Association, 1980), pp. 16–17, for a brief review of this subject and for references to the technical literature. Nowadays, biologists are fairly well agreed upon calling the bear a hibernator.

43. Brookes, R., *The Natural History of Quadrupeds* (London, 1768), p. 195.

44. O'Neill, J.W., *Glimpses of Animated Nature* (Philadelphia: Charles DeSilber & Sons, 1878), p. 88.

45. Thrasher, Halsey, *The Hunter and Trapper* (New York: Orange Judd, 1868), p. 51. As in so many cases, misconceptions in early natural history had some basis in fact. The common hibernation position of the bear often places the paws near the mouth; American Indians also observed what they thought was paw-sucking, and there is no reason why paw-sucking might not occasionally occur. To add yet another twist to the story, a recent research project revealed that black bears sometimes shed the outer pad of their paw during hibernation, and eat the pads upon awakening (Lynn Rogers, "Shedding of Foot Pads by Black Bears During Denning," *Journal of Mammalogy*, Vol. 55, No. 3, pp. 672–74).

46. E.T. Bennett, ed., *The Gardens and Menagerie of the Zoological Society Delineated* (London: Thomas Tegg, 1830), pp. 104–5.

47. If there was a mystery that captured the imagination of early naturalists as much as hibernation it was the absolutely bewildering fact that "no man, either Christian or Indian, ever killed a She-Bear with young" (Brickell, *History of North Carolina*, as quoted in George Douglas, "On the Natural History of the *Ursus Americanus*; or *American Black Bear*," *Transactions of the Literary and Historical Society of Quebec*, Vol. 4, Part I, 1843, p. 60). Of all the thousands of bears hunted and killed in Europe and North America, writers virtually never encountered a pregnant female.

Bears usually give birth in January or February, quite some time before emergence from the den (often emergence does not occur until late April or May). Because hunters, tracking or trapping free-ranging animals in summer and fall, never found a pregnant female, it was widely assumed that bears mated right before denning (or, as Topsell asserted, all winter long). By the mid-1800s scientists had observed bear mating habits in zoos, and had established that mating did occur in June and July, but that only deepened the mystery. Under that set of dates, a sow bear killed in October should have been carrying a substantial fetus (Douglas, above, believed that the "coupling season" was in September. Arthur Baker, "A Notable Success in the Breeding of Black Bears," *Smithsonian Miscellaneous Collections*, Vol. 45, 1904, pp. 175–79, outlined the twelve-year mating history of a pair of black bears in a private zoo in Ohio, and further reported on successful matings in the 1890s in zoos in Washington, D.C. and Springfield, Massachusetts).

The answer to this puzzle had to wait until modern biologists conducted microscopic examinations of the bear's reproductive tract. Bears, like a few other animals, have adapted to their feast-and-famine cycle through a process known as embryonic delay. Basically this involves a fertilized ova that goes into a sort of holding pattern for several months; it stops growing almost immediately after fertilization, when it consists of only a few cells. Late in the fall, three or more months after mating, something in the bear's metabolism triggers the start of growth in the embryo, which then implants itself in the uterine wall and resumes normal growth. The beauty of the process is almost poetic. All during the heaviest feeding season the sow bear is feeding only herself, storing up fat for winter. About the time she dens up, her embryo begins to grow, so that though the total gestation period is rather more than seven months the fetus has only been actively developing for half that time (and remains so small as to be invisible to casual autopsy until early winter). Thus, the newborn cubs are born, as we were told by Topsell, "no bigger than rats." In their small size (for contrast, compare a 250-pound bear mother with a one-pound baby to a 120-pound human mother with a six-pound baby) we find the real beauty of embryonic delay. If the mother had carried out a normal full-term pregnancy, she would give birth to cubs weighing fifteen pounds each. Their nutritional needs would be quite unmanageable. When they are born she has at least two more months of confinement ahead of her, and they must survive (as must she) on what nourishment her system has to provide. Born the size of squirrels, their needs are very small, so that during their first two months of life in the den they complete their "prenatal growth." They emerge with their mother in spring weighing about ten pounds each (see Arthur Pearson, *The Northern Interior Grizzly Bear*, Canadian Wildlife Service Report Series, Number 34, 1975, for a review of literature on embryonic delay in grizzly bears).

Of course the existence and mechanics of embryonic delay weren't even suspected in Roosevelt's time, but scientists were far ahead of popular writers, especially hunting writers, in understanding mating behavior and schedule.

48. There are several popular books that review the early literature of grizzly bear/man encounters. For French Canadian trappers, Lewis and Clark, and the early mountain men, see Harold McCracken, *The Beast That Walks Like Man* (New York: Hanover House, 1955), Andy Russell, *Grizzly Country* (New York: Alfred Knopf, 1967), and Haynes and Haynes, *The Grizzly Bear: Portraits From Life* (Norman: University of Oklahoma Press, 1966). For the early Spanish encounters, see Storer and Tevis, *California Grizzly* (Berkeley: University of California Press, 1955).

49. Steve Herrero, "Aspects of Evolution and Adaptation in American Black Bears (*Ursus americanus* Pallas) and brown and grizzly bears (*U. arctos* Linne) of North America," in Steve Herrero, ed., *Bears, Their Biology and Management* (Morges, Switzerland: International Union for the Conservation of Nature, 1972, pp. 221–31). This source, and Bjorn Kurten, *The Cave Bear Story* (New York: Columbia University Press, 1976), trace the evolution of the modern grizzly bear and the modern black bear from a common European ancestor. The relevant point is that the grizzly, as it became a more open-country animal than its ancestral tree-climbing bear, developed different habits to deal with the new circumstances. Black bears, which retained most of the habits of the common ancestor, are dependent on trees for refuge, often even as adults. When grizzlies forsook the forest, they no longer had such a refuge, and no longer had a sure place to send their young in time of danger. It is the belief of modern bear scientists that the lack of a nearby refuge, either for self or young, was a major contributing factor

in the grizzly becoming a far more aggressive and belligerent animal. Perhaps by the same token, grizzlies that ranged for countless generations over the open prairie in search of bison became more aggressive than grizzlies that lived more regularly in the proximity of heavy forest.

50. For one example, the Yellowstone Park grizzly management controversy, see Paul Schullery, *The Bears of Yellowstone*.

51. One notion that many non-hunters have difficulty with is that an animal's chance of survival is sometimes improved if it is classified as a game animal and made available for hunting. Once it is so classified, it falls under the jurisdiction of a government agency—possibly several—and the agency must then learn enough about the animal to establish reasonable limits and control the harvest. Until it reaches that point, in some cases, it has no protection at all.

Unfortunately there are still a number of people living in and around bear country who think of bears as worthless varmints. Remaining grizzly populations in the lower forty-eight are subjected to varying degrees of poaching and simple vandalism-killings.

52. McCracken, Russell, Haynes, and Storer and Tevis, above, all recount the destruction of the grizzly.

53. Though there will for a long time be several thousand grizzlies in Alaska and Canada, many modern grizzly defenders agree with Aldo Leopold, who once said that "relegating grizzlies to Alaska is about like relegating happiness to Heaven; one may never get there."

54. Storer and Tevis, *California Grizzly*, pp. 8–9.

55. C. Hart Merriam, "Review of the Grizzly and Big Brown Bears of North America," *North American Fauna No. 41* (Washington: U.S. Government Printing Office, 1918).

56. Cutright, *Roosevelt the Naturalist*, pp. 80–85.

57. Theodore Roosevelt, "A Layman's Views on Specific Nomenclature," *Science*, Vol. V, No. 122, April 30, 1897. This article was only part of the exchange that took place at the time between Merriam and Roosevelt. See Cutright, pp. 80–85, for more detail.

58. Cutright, *Roosevelt the Naturalist*, p. 82.

59. See also George Bird Grinnell, "North American Bears," *Forest and Stream*, May 2, 1896, p. 1, and Arthur Erwin Brown, "Species of North American Bears," *Forest and Stream*, December 16, 1893, pp. 518–19, for contrasting opinions on bear speciation.

60. Morison, *Letters*, I:612.

61. Roosevelt estimated (in Chapter Six here) that the first grizzly he killed weighed around 1,200 pounds, and we can wonder if that was not an exuberant overestimate. In a letter home at the time he said it weighed "over a thousand pounds." In either

case it would have been an unusually large grizzly. It was not only the first he'd shot, it was the first he'd ever seen in the wild; I realize that I am not the skilled observer Roosevelt was, but the first grizzly *I* ever saw in the wild weighed, for that first moment or so, about six tons. Dead weight of something as spectacular as a grizzly bear is very hard to estimate.

62. Cutright, *Roosevelt the Naturalist*, p. 54.

63. Scientists involved in capturing bear cubs have noted that the mother can often be frightened away. On the other hand, sows with young are statistically the most likely to injure a human who encounters them.

64. See Schullery, *The Bears of Yellowstone*, pp. 46–47, for a review of some scientific studies of sow-cub relationships.

65. See especially Chapter Three, "The Bear's Disposition."

66. A thorough study of known incidents involving grizzly bears and humans is Steve Herrero, "Conflicts Between Man and Grizzly Bears in the National Parks of North America," in Pelton, Lentfer, and Folk, eds., *Bears, Their Biology and Management* (Morges, Switzerland: International Union for the Conservation of Nature, 1976), pp. 121–46. Several studies are now underway in national parks to determine ways to reduce the chance of injury by better understanding the bear.

67. McCracken, *The Beast That Walks Like Man* and Russell, *Grizzly Country*. For this book, all references to the grizzly have been changed to the modern form.

INDEX

Index

Index

Index

Index

Paul Schullery is a historian of the American conservation movement. For several years he worked in Yellowstone National Park as a ranger-naturalist and as park archivist, and since 1977 he has been executive director of The Museum of American Fly Fishing in Manchester, Vermont. He is a member of the Association of Interpretive Naturalists, the Association of National Park Rangers, the Society of American Archivists, the Theodore Roosevelt Association, and numerous conservation organizations. His articles and reviews have appeared in several journals and magazines, and his previous books include *Old Yellowstone Days* (Colorado Associated University Press, 1979), *The Bears of Yellowstone* (Yellowstone Library and Museum Association, 1980), and *The Grand Canyon: Early Impressions* (Colorado Associated University Press, 1981).

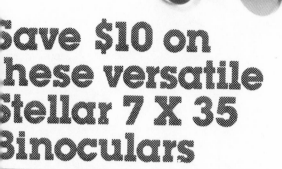